RON *and* LIB LOFTIS

A Marriage for the Ages

KARL W. MERRITT

ISBN: 979-8-89090-611-3 (sc)
ISBN: 979-8-89090-612-0 (hb)
ISBN: 979-8-89090-613-7 (e)

EXPRESSO
Executive Center 777, Dunsmuir Street Vancouver, BC V71K4
1-888-721-0662 ext 101
info@expressopublishing.com

Dedication

To all who wish for, dream of, success in marriage.

Cover Designed By
Holly Elizabeth Obermiller
Granddaughter of Ron and Lib Loftis

CONTENTS

INTRODUCTION

Across all of my growing-up years, I looked forward to getting married and having a family. I envisioned having all of the wonderful experiences that were not part of my childhood years. I longed for the simple things like sitting with family and watching a television show. Now, after 77 years of living, I lament that my greatest childhood dream never happened.

However, some four or five years ago, I met Ron and Lib Loftis. As I write this introduction, Ron is 92 and Lib is 91. They have been married over 70 years. My first recognition of them was when they came up together in a church conference to report on the prayer effort that they were leading. I was interested in what they had to say about the Monday prayer time, but more struck by the love and oneness that was so obvious between them.

Given the difficulties of my marital journey, I was amazed by what I saw in them, just in those few minutes. I joined their prayer group and over the next several years got to watch them together and interact with them. Finally, it hit me that they had built a tremendously successful marriage. Given that observation and absolute conclusion, I asked if they would allow me to tell their story in a book. Thankfully, they agreed.

Over almost a year, we met and talked about their journey from being in high school together to a love-filled marriage that is clearly "A Marriage for the Ages". That time with them was eye-opening, also revealing as to how I would have been helped tremendously if I could have had time with them early in my married life. However, even after my lifetime of being married, I was helped by time with Ron and Lib.

Consequently, I am sharing their story in the hope that others will be helped by it as they navigate preparing for marriage or being in a marriage.

Karl W. Merritt

CHAPTER ONE

WHY THIS BOOK?

"A successful marriage is generally defined as a dynamic and growing relationship in which both partners continue to develop and achieve personal satisfaction."[1]

Throughout this book, "successful marriage(s)" appears often. There is also mention of "joy" and "happiness" in marriage. Where "successful marriage(s)" appears, it is being used as defined in the quote above. Further, I see "joy" and "happiness" as being present, a kind of by-product, when a marriage is successful. Even further, there are other very positive outcomes from these marriages. Among those are strong family relationships, children who are prepared for independent living as adults, and so forth. The aim of this book is to share the life journey of a couple that has achieved great success in marriage. My hope is that others will be helped in their marriage by reading this account of a "Marriage for the Ages."

Mine has been a challenging marriage journey. My first marriage ended in divorce after about three years. My second wife died of cancer after 17 years of marriage. After almost 33 years into my current marriage, my wife and I, over recent years, have settled into a good relationship that still has challenges at times. I contend that a fact of life is that relationships of every kind are difficult; though particularly true of marriage.

In my second marriage, we briefly tried family counseling. That effort collapsed after a few sessions. The collapse was due, in great part, to me not agreeing with some of what the therapist was calling on me to do. Furthermore, it did not help that we were moved from a therapist whom I felt was effective to one whose approach I found off-putting and combative.

My current wife and I completed intensive pre-marital counseling and, in the mid-1990s, spent months in sessions with a very capable marriage and family therapist. That investment was not nearly as helpful as it could have been if I had been more forthcoming regarding the course of my life and the impact of negative events and experiences along the way.

The bottom line is that my marriages have not nearly been what I hoped for and expected in marriage and family. More importantly, three women have been denied the happiness and joy that a successful marriage should make possible. My current wife has spent almost 33 years joined with me in pursuit of the happiness and joy that marriage should bring. Even though the goal seems in sight at times, we never quite get there and remain in a state of pursuit.

After what seemed like a lifetime of being married, I pretty much concluded that marriage is a rollercoaster of good days and bad, valleys and mountaintops; more bad days than good, more valleys than mountaintops. I aimed to settle into a mode of being thankful for the good days and mountaintops while working to survive the bad days and valleys.

Then, in approximately 2018, as I was taking on this new mode for dealing with marriage, I was attending a Wednesday night church conference at the church where I am a member in Fayetteville, North Carolina. Ronald (Ron) and Lib Loftis were called to the microphone to report on a prayer group that they were leading in the church. Both of them were in their mid-80s at the time. As I start this chapter on 1 January 2024, Ron is 92 and Lib is 90 and they have been married over 71 years. They stood and talked about the prayer group that was meeting on Mondays at noon. As I listened, I was encouraged by, and attracted to, the effort that they were describing. What commanded my attention even more was the obvious love and oneness of purpose between the two of them.

I sat there thinking: "These people have figured out and acted on what it takes to be successful, to be happy and productive, in marriage." Not because of the marriage piece, but because I felt moved by the Holy Spirit to do so, I joined that prayer group and, to this day, hardly miss a Monday meeting.

Over the next three or four years, being in those prayer meetings allowed me to observe Ron and Lib as they led those times of prayer. They were a team and the love between them was so obvious. After they gave up leadership of the group, they would sit there side-by-side, sometimes speaking to one another in tones and with words that screamed love and togetherness. Across the years, and to this day, on Mondays, we often arrive in the parking lot at the same time. I get to watch as Ron opens the car door for Lib and they walk into the church with her holding his arm and Ron navigating with his cane.

Simply watching them awakened me to what marriage should and can be. For me, and for the millions of others like me who desire, but struggle, to build sound marriages, I believe that God assigned me to tell Ron and Lib's marital story. Thankfully, they agreed to allow me to tell that story.

Over the course of several months, we met and talked about their journey and recorded those sessions. I know that the account of their marriage journey can be of tremendous value and provide much needed help to couples and individuals who want to be successful in marriage. I know this to be true because I have been helped and blessed beyond measure by sitting in their presence and hearing how they built what is clearly **"A Marriage for the Ages"**.

In all of my nearly 77 years of living, until time with Ron and Lib, I had never had profound external prompting to self-examination, along with identifying and seeking, to take on attitudes and actions that are clearly essential to success in marriage.

For instance, I am coming to grips with how I was adversely affected by the turmoil in my parents' marriage. Individually, my mother and father were wonderful parents. However, the constant tension between them made my growing-up years very difficult. They divorced after a little over 20 years of marriage, but not before I was in college and moving on in life. In all of my therapy sessions and struggles in marriages, I never gave due attention to how living through those years of my parents' unhealthy marriage adversely impacted me. I loved and respected both of them beyond what words can express. They prepared me to be successful in all that life has thrown at me, except for marriage.

Ron and Lib did not hear my story of growing up with the tension between my mother and father and then explain to me how I was adversely affected by it. Rather, I was able to walk through that process on my own because they were open and honest regarding the grappling with their own personal life experiences that challenged success in their marriage.

Along with accounts of challenges they faced and overcame, simply hearing their remembrances of events and experiences across 70+ years of what has proved to be a very successful marriage, provides instruction for success in marriage. With every fiber of my being, I believe that statement to be true. Therein is the answer to "Why This Book?"

Let the record be clear: I make no claim of educational background or professional experience that provide me with expertise in addressing the building of a successful marriage. I am simply a man who has failed to, in my own marriage, achieve the success that I now know is possible. I know it because God blessed me with time in the presence of Ron and Lib Loftis. My aim is to share with others the lessons gleaned from that still ongoing experience.

I will forever thank God for this amazing experience and the opportunity to share it with others.

CHAPTER TWO

BEGINNING THE JOURNEY TO TRUE LOVE

Without doubt, love must abound if a marriage is to be successful. A major problem in the arena of love is that everything that looks like love is not genuine. In our time, much of what is referred to as love is far from it. The Apostle Paul, in 1 Corinthians 13:4-7 (New King James), describes love:

> ***4 Love suffers long and is kind; love does not envy; love does not parade itself, is not [b] puffed up; 5 does not behave rudely, does not seek its own, is not provoked, [c]thinks no evil; 6 does not rejoice in iniquity, but rejoices in the truth; 7 bears all things, believes all things, hopes all things, endures all things.***

No couple, no person, simply stumbles into the state of being that is described above. This is true love and people everywhere would do well to pursue it. My experience says that only having the will to do so is not sufficient for success. Will and desire are important, but instruction and exposure to successful models of true love are essential. This truth regarding instruction and successful models did not hit me clearly until I spent time watching and talking with Lib and Ron Loftis. In the hope that their journey to true love will instruct and provide a useful and successful model, what follows is a word picture of the start of their journey.

That journey to true love and an extremely successful marriage started when they met while attending the same high school in Hope Mills, North Carolina. Ron and his brother, Myron, were in the same class. Lib was two years behind them. She had heard about Ron from her sister and others who reported that he was studious and liked by the teachers. Teachers saw something valuable and promising in him. Further, she learned that Ron played on the school's football and basketball teams.

Likewise, Ron was aware of Lib; although they had never met. He was attracted to her in a "boy/girl kind of thing". However, while describing her as "pretty", he speaks more at length regarding her having a "decent personality and good reputation". Lib says, and Ron confirms, that from the beginning and across all these years of marriage, Ron is absolutely attracted to her "big brown eyes". After almost 71 years of marriage, Ron says he still gets "butterflies" when he looks at Lib.

Their first meeting happened after a football game in which Ron was playing quarterback. Ron's team was not very good. However, they scored a touchdown in that game. Lib says the players on Ron's team were "mill boys" and did not do the physical work of their competitors who lived on farms and did heavy manual labor. There were textile mills in the Fayetteville area where Ron and his teammates lived. Consequently, they were not exposed to the physically demanding work that comes with farming.

Despite scoring a touchdown, Ron's team lost the game. After the game, Lib saw Ron looking dejected as he walked across the field. She said to him, "Well, don't look so discouraged; at least we scored a touchdown tonight." Ron's response was to ask, "Can I take you home?" He was riding with his brother, Sonny, in his crème-colored 1941 Oldsmobile car. Knowing that her father would strongly disapprove of her riding alone with Ron and the other boys who were with him, she asked a friend if she would ride with them. The friend agreed and so started an amazing journey.

This relationship did not start with a "big bang". In the early stages, they did not talk so much about being a couple. They shared their individual dreams for the future. For instance, Lib told Ron that she would like to have four children. Though Ron heard that, he did not give much thought to the statement because they were just talking, sharing hopes and dreams. Additionally, Ron's father was not one who talked with his sons about sexual matters. Consequently, Lib's desire to have four children did not grab Ron's attention.

However, on their second or third date, Ron asked Lib if he may kiss her. Of note is the fact that he asked. There was no assumption on his part that he could simply invade her space.

As Ron and Lib started their relationship, there was a hiccup. Lib went to a Halloween carnival at the school and realized that Ron was there with her sister as his date. Lib remembers thinking, "There is my fella with my sister." However, she was not angry with Ron because she knew that her sister liked to "one-up her". Her sister could have said "no" to Ron's invitation, but did not.

After seeing them at the carnival, Lib thought that was the end of the matter. However, that was not the end. The school newspaper ran an article with the headline, "What sister will I date next?" Lib was able to accurately and calmly analyze that event and move on. Even as a young teenager, she had the capacity for reasoning with clarity while obviously putting aside emotions that would have hindered clearly thinking through an embarrassing, and even insulting, experience.

In addition to football, Ron played basketball. Lib was a cheerleader for both sports. Consequently, they shared going to ballgames. For them, that was a point of common interest; having that common interest helped cement their relationship.

Then there was what might, especially in today's society, be a throw-away, a meaningless gesture. Since there was no air conditioning in their school, classroom doors were left open. Ron would, somehow, get out of his class and appear outside the door of one of Lib's classrooms; the same one every time. Once he got her attention, he would wink, she would smile, and her heart would race. As she describes that experience, there is a gentle laugh and a natural smile that fills her face.

For Ron, an immensely impactful experience in the bonding process between them came when Ron's brother, Sonny, died at a very young age. With obvious emotion, Ron talks about how Lib was there for him in that very difficult time. He was still in high school when Sonny died. Her support had a profoundly positive impact on Ron and, for him, helped move their relationship to a more serious level. Neither of them dated anybody else after going through that experience together.

On 26 November 1948, Ron asked Lib to "go steady". In that time, this was viewed as the step just prior to becoming engaged. Their relationship continued as Ron graduated from high school and went off to college at North Carolina State University. His college career lasted a year and a half. He loved and missed Lib. That combination of loving and missing her led him to leave college and marry Lib. They married two weeks after Lib's nineteenth birthday; Ron was twenty.

This was the beginning of a "marriage for the ages"; clearly conceived on the foundation of 1 Corinthians 13:4-7.

CHAPTER THREE

TOGETHER WITH GOD

"Believing is not just a 'concept', it produces action. When we believe we speak, we obey, we do."[1]

All the way back to their youth, across many years, Ron and Lib Loftis have walked closely with God. For them, that element of their marriage and living has consistently remained central and essential. They give God credit and thanks for His faithfulness in good times and in those that were not so good.

Lib's journey to faith in and reliance on God started when she was just a youngster. During World War II, a man came to her home recruiting people to sell packets of vegetable seeds. If a person sold 10 packets, they received a picture Bible storybook. Even though she was not good at selling, Lib signed on to sell seeds. She managed to sell eight packets and her mother purchased the remaining two packets.

With excitement, she received and started reading the picture Bible storybook. The more she read, the more she wanted to read. That selling and reading experience started her on a life-long close walk with God.

Lib's family lived in Cumberland Mill Village, less than a mile from Cumberland Baptist Church. Along with her mother and sister, she attended that church on a regular basis. Her father did not attend. She and her sister became very active in the church, including Lib teaching a Sunday school class of young children. Further, the two sisters faithfully participated in a Wednesday night Bible study that mostly included young people.

Given that this starting point was many years ago, the joy and glow with which Lib gives the account of this introduction to faith speaks volumes regarding the tremendous positive impact of it on her. Her face lights up and her voice projects happiness when she tells of her mother teaching her the song "Away in a Manger" even before Lib could read. The foundation for faith was laid and laid well.

Ron's journey to faith was not immediate or very direct. He was born in Indianapolis, Indiana and lived there until 1941. That was the year his father accepted a job at Fort Bragg in Fayetteville, North Carolina. He was 10 years old at the time of the move to North Carolina.

Ron remembers very little about going to church in Indianapolis. However, he has a certificate from Speedway Boulevard Methodist Church dated April 28, 1935. Apparently, there was some church involvement by his family, but Ron did not start a journey to faith during that time. At some point after their arrival in Fayetteville, his family started attending Big Rockfish Presbyterian Church.

Pursuing a faith relationship with God did not genuinely commence until high school when Ron started dating Lib and attending worship and other church activities with her. In the fall of 1949, Lib was a junior in high school. Their dating was limited by lack of funds and because Lib's parents did not allow going to the movies on Sundays. They spent Sunday mornings and evenings in church.[2]

The primary impediment to Ron entering a faith relationship with God through Jesus Christ was his questioning how God could allow three very painful events in his life. These will be addressed in greater detail later. Here is what Ron writes in "An Unfinished Story: A Family History from October 7, 1939 through June 30, 2007":

> ***"During the fall of 1949 I had been attending church a good bit and was trying to make some sense of Religion, Church, God, Jesus Christ, etc. I had not been able to work through the question of why a loving God that Christians talked about would want to 'take' my loved ones from me. As a kid I believed God had 'taken' my mother. Then, I understood the preacher to say that God 'took' Johnny Rasmusson, and later he 'took' my brother Sonny at the young age of 19. It seemed to me the preachers were always saying, 'It is God's Will.' How could I trust a God to love me if he was always taking away from me all the persons that I loved so much? In time I came to understand that God was not 'taking' those persons from me: he was 'receiving' them into His Heaven when something tragic happened here on earth. Jesus Christ was/is the one who makes it possible for us to be received into heaven when these tragic things happen. When I was able to see that, then my heart opened up to Christ and I was able to accept him and receive salvation. It was that November in the year 1949, at age 18 that I professed faith in Jesus Christ and, in early 1950 I was baptized and became a member of the Cumberland Baptist Church. That was a turning point in my life."***[3]

Ron's coming to faith was, in great part, nurtured by his attending worship and Wednesday night youth activities with Lib.

He writes the following regarding coming to grips with his feelings for her:

> ***"...in November 1948 I was convinced I wanted Libby to be more than my steady girlfriend. I had grown up feeling that nothing I ever had stayed with me very long. It seemed that I was always losing whatever I got close to. With Libby I seldom had that feeling. Only on those few occasions when we differed about some issue or when I thought she was paying more attention to something or someone other than me did I get that 'losing' feeling. I sensed about Libby that she felt toward me as I felt toward her. Because she was so pretty and so charming and so outgoing I always had that latent fear of losing her. I was so insecure I felt the words of the song, 'I'd rather have a Paper Doll' made popular by the Ames Brothers were written just for me. I know now that it was more my doing that created those feelings. But for many years I did not know that."***[4]

After graduating from high school, Ron decided not to go to college. He worked a couple of jobs as well as enrolling in the International Correspondence School to study architecture. After working for a short time, Ron's father offered to provide financial help for him to attend college. Ron enrolled at North Carolina State University in Raleigh, North Carolina. That first year went well. All was also well with him and Lib. Ron made regular weekend trips home and spent the bulk of that time with her.

Then came the trip home when Lib told Ron that she thought she was pregnant. Here is what Ron wrote regarding his reaction to Lib's announcement:

> ***"The emotions that revelation caused are too numerous to list but, I will mention a few. There was fear. What do we do now? How do we handle this? What will Libby's family and her church think? There was guilt. I think both of us felt guilt. I did, because I was responsible for ruining the reputation of a truly Christian girl. I felt guilt because I had hurt the person I loved more dearly than anyone I had ever loved. I felt guilt because I knew it was my fault and I had taken advantage of true love that Libby had for me. I also felt shame. Her family had trusted me and she had trusted me. I had made a profession of faith in Christ just a year earlier and now I had broken the trust God had placed in me."***[5]

I submit that Ron's words, as quoted above, show the thought process of people who are in a real relationship with God through Jesus Christ. I encourage the reader to read that quoted section again. There is, in America, an effort to bring people to right actions through man-made laws, governmental programs, restrictions on constitutionally protected rights, manipulation of thought for political gain, and even suppression of religion. That list is just a miniscule sampling of what is going on in the name of doing what is good for people in our country.

Ron's words and, later, actions, along with Lib's words and actions, show that they assessed their situation in light of what God demanded of them in their living. I contend that despite their momentary, but serious, turn from God's will and how God responded provides a lesson for us all. The lesson is that relationship with God and a genuine desire/effort to live as He calls us to live is the only path to authentic joy, peace, and a truly successful life. For me, the measure of success in life is the extent to which a person answers the call of God on his or her life. The truth of that statement shows through clearly in the remaining pages of this book. The other fact that shows through is God's amazing willingness and capacity to use us for good even when we see ourselves as broken and beyond God's reach.

Ron writes about how, despite his panic, he started to think through what he and Lib should do. Without doubt, these were thoughts prompted by and based in a real relationship with God.

> ***"In the midst of my emotions I began to panic. I knew the only reasonable choice was marriage. Abortion was not a consideration. Nor was sending Libby off to have the baby. We never considered any option but marriage. We saw no way we could talk to anyone else about it, and while I did not feel the need to do that I feared I was making it harder on Libby. I knew also that I had to return to college and complete the term which would end in late March. She would continue working at the Bakery and we would try to act as if nothing had happened.***
>
> ***You must remember that unmarried girls in the 1950s did not have access to pregnancy tests as they do today. A girl having a child out of wedlock was a disgrace to her and to her family. And especially to my children you must know and believe me when I say that the pregnancy was not the result of loose morals or hot passion. It came from a growing feeling of love that could not be satisfied by holding hands, talking or kissing. There were deeply seated emotions of love that could not be satisfied in any other way. At one point, months before she was pregnant, we had talked about staying away from each other for an extended period***

> ***of time to see if this would pass. But we never followed up on that. I am sure others have loved each other as strongly as we did but I cannot see how anyone could love MORE than we did."[6]***

Without telling either set of parents or anybody else about the pregnancy, Ron and Lib planned a wedding. They were married on April 12, 1952. Lib's parents accepted the marriage, but Ron's father did not. He had made it clear to Ron that he would provide financial help for him to attend college as long as he did not get married. His father kept to that promise. Despite having to give up college, Ron stood up and did what he knew to be right and what love demanded.

In my estimation, the record is clear; God kept His hand on Ron and Lib. Leaving college after that first year, through a friend, Ron got a job with the North Carolina Highway and Public Works Department. He and Lib moved into a homemade trailer with one bedroom and one bath. The monthly rent was $20.00. They had very little money left over after paying bills and buying groceries. At one point, they collected drink bottles and turned them in for the deposits, attempting to "make ends meet".

Across 72 years of marriage, despite challenges and difficult times, they were faithful to God and God was faithful to them. Here is the "big picture" of that journey:

1. Became parents to four children; three boys and a girl.
2. Progressed from a homemade trailer to comfortable homes; including the one that is their place of retirement.
3. Ron holds a Doctor of Ministry while Lib has a master's degree.
4. Of their four children, one holds a Master of Business Administration (MBA), one a Bachelor of Science (BS) in Civil Engineering, another a Doctor of Ministry, and

the fourth has two master's degrees, one of which is in Counseling. All of these children are financially self-supporting and generous in caring for their parents.

5. The successful focus on education has continued to grandchildren. Ron and Lib have nine grandchildren. Seven of the nine have completed college degrees, one of the remaining two is early in his college career, while the ninth will graduate high school in 2025. The high schooler has received invitations to attend several colleges when he graduates.
6. After working with the North Carolina Highway and Public Works Department for 16 years, Ron accepted the call to ministry. In the beginning of his service as a pastor, his income was about half of what it had been with the previous job. Despite the pay-cut, they survived and were faithful to live out Ron's call to ministry.
7. Ron served twice as Pastor of Lake Lynn Baptist Church in Fayetteville, NC. In fact, he retired from active pastoring during his second period of service. He also worked eight years at New South River Baptist Association in Fayetteville as Director of Christian Social Ministries. He spent 18 months in Atlanta, Georgia, working with the Home Mission Board of the Southern Baptist Convention. That was followed by eight years as Director of Missions for the Robeson Baptist Association in Lumberton, North Carolina. Ron taught at the University of North Carolina Pembroke.
8. Lib taught in Fayetteville, North Carolina area public schools for 30 years until retirement. She also completed training to employ the Laubach method in teaching reading and taught reading in many places across many years. She also taught religious classes in many churches,

played piano and directed choirs, and was very active in the Woman's Missionary Union (WMU).

9. In what is supposed to be retirement, they each teach Sunday school classes at First Baptist Church on Anderson Street in Fayetteville; both have served as deacons in that Church. In fact, Lib had a term as Chair of Deacons.
10. Ron and Lib Loftis are partners in ministry in a fashion that sets the "Gold Standard" for what such a joint effort should look like and be.

The listing above is intended to give some feel for the amazingly powerful way that God has used, and continues to use this couple; to do so despite their early failure to follow God's will and the feelings of guilt resulting from that failure. A key step in regaining our balance and moving on with answering God's call after failing Him is to recognize that He is still with us; to see His hand in the day-to-day happenings of life. The need for, and the effect of, recognizing God's faithfulness shows through in Ron and Lib's journey.

The listing of instances where God showed up for this couple and they recognized His showing up is almost limitless. The next few paragraphs highlight some of these experiences where God made known His presence.

Lib spent the first 13 years of their marriage as a stay-at-home mother. She had talked about going to college, but never took the steps to do so. One day, Ron suggested to her that she should enroll. Shortly thereafter, the two of them met with the registrar at the University of North Carolina Pembroke. The registrar explained that an application would normally be required from Lib before considering her for admission. Without the application in place, she was allowed to immediately take the Scholastic Aptitude Test (SAT) within a matter of days. After being out of high school for years and having made no preparation for taking the test, she scored well and was accepted into college. Lib went on to earn her undergraduate degree in two years and nine months.

Early in his ministry, Ron was called to pastor a church near Fayetteville. Around March 1969, a situation presented itself when he recommended holding a joint Vacation Bible School with the two other churches in that town; one of them being a Black congregation. This experience is addressed in greater detail in a later chapter. In response to reported division in the membership because of this matter, Ron resigned as Pastor rather than jeopardize the continued existence of that church.

Given that he had also resigned his employment with the State of North Carolina, the decision to leave the church left him with no income. Although Lib had started working as a teacher, teachers were not paid two months during the summer. They were facing a summer with no employment income.

The last Sunday in June 1969 would be the end of his pastorate at the church where he had resigned. Before that Sunday, the pulpit committee from Clybonville Baptist Church in Lumberton, North Carolina met with Ron and Lib. They invited Ron to serve as their interim pastor. He had been recommended by I. Ruth Martin, a religion teacher at Pembroke College.[7] Ron wrote the following regarding her comments to him regarding dealing with this congregation and with people in general:

> ***"'These are good people, Ronald. They are truly Christians, but remember that they are human beings also and sometimes our human nature takes over before our Christian nature kicks in.' That statement has helped me out of many dilemmas I have had with Christians over my 40 years of ministry.[8]***

The Clybonville Baptist Church congregation could not pay Ron very much monetarily, but they cared for the Loftis family in a fashion still greatly appreciated and celebrated by Ron and Lib. Over the course of that meager income summer, the members of that church gave this family more vegetables than they could eat. There was very little by way of food that they had to purchase; maybe ingredients for making bread and meat for seasoning the vegetables. Every time they went to church, there would be a bag of vegetables. There was so much that some had to be frozen.

As a reminder, Ron was the interim pastor at this church. However, he saw indicators that there was interest in calling him to serve as pastor. Recognizing this, he requested a meeting with the Pastor Search Committee and explained to them that if they were considering him, he did not feel that God was leading him to serve as pastor. He encouraged them to move on with their search efforts. As much as Ron and Lib loved and appreciated the membership, they also realized that they could not financially afford to serve that church.

On the very next Sunday after Ron's meeting with the Pastor Search Committee, there were five men from Lake Lynn Baptist Church sitting on the back row in the morning worship service. They were on the Pastor Search Committee for their church. In the process started by that visit, Ron was called as pastor at Lake Lynn. He served there eight years the first time and, after leaving for other opportunities, returned to serve 12 additional years.

Be reminded that these are two people who recognized, and still recognize, the importance of education and therefore made it a priority for themselves and for their children. Reflect on this fact: From 1968 to 1984, there was only one year when there was not a member of the household in college. Even further, when their four children completed their undergraduate degrees that Ron and Lib committed to finance, there were no loans that had been engaged and not a single institution was owed a penny.

These accounts of God's faithfulness are almost endless. Consequently, here is a final one:

> ***Ron speaking..."I was working at my computer one Monday night doing some final things for my class at Pembroke on Tuesday morning. It was March 2020. I fell out of my computer chair onto the floor. She was in the den, which is halfway through the house. She heard the thud and came in. Essentially, I had to go to the hospital. They had to delay surgery because they found some infection somewhere. Finally, they did the surgery to put a pacemaker in. In putting in the pacemaker, they were about to close up shop when one of the men saw that my heart was bleeding. So they had to open up my chest and put two stitches in my heart then close back up. That was in March during spring break at Pembroke. So that was a good time for that kind of thing to happen. Then, in May, two months later, there was an infection, and the result was there was fluid gathering up here (the head). So, I went in and had neurosurgery done on the brain."***

The need for neurosurgery on the brain was discovered when Ron was back home after having the pacemaker implanted and became unsteady on his feet. He was transported to the hospital. Late that night, the surgery was completed. It turned out that fluid was on both sides of his head, but they could only clear one side at the time. Consequently, the one side was cleared and the doctor explained that they would monitor the other side and if it did not clear, additional surgery would be required.

Over the next few months, Ron underwent CT scans to check that remaining fluid-filled side. Each scan was followed by a visit with the surgeon. The fluid was diminishing a little at a time. The doctor repeated that if the fluid did not drain, they would have to perform another surgery. In August, Lib and Ron went in for an appointment with the surgeon. The surgeon came in, went over, and sat down. He said, "Well, it was a miracle. That fluid is gone. I have no explanation for it, except it was a miracle. Have you been praying?"

Then the surgeon sat there and told them about multiple instances where, if God had not intervened, he would have lost the patient. He said he was doing some delicate surgery on a little girl and his hands were so big that he expected difficulty getting to the site. However, he did not have a bit of trouble. His hands went straight to where they needed to be. He said, "It was a miracle."

Ron and Lib Loftis were thankful for their miracle and they fully recognized God as the source of that miracle. Across hours of my recorded conversations with this couple in preparation for writing this book, they repeatedly made it crystal clear that whatever good that has come to them was provided by God who loves them. These statements were not mere sound-good proclamations. Time and time again, even when there was risk and sacrifice involved, they answered God's call, trusted Him, and God kept showing up.

If an individual does not read beyond this chapter, leave with the clear understanding, totally recognizing, that a truly successful marriage is only possible where there is right relationship with God through Jesus Christ. In that relationship, God does not give up on us when we fall short of His will. Instead, He stays nearby, calling us to make walking in His way our goal and being blessed as we do so. Ron and Lib's journey testifies to the truth of this being what God offers us. Let it be that we learn from them.

CHAPTER FOUR

COMING TO GRIPS

"If you say that someone has a grip on reality, you mean they recognize the true situation and do not have mistaken ideas about it."[1]

My view is that failure in coming to grips with the reality of challenging, of painful, situations and conditions is an occurrence in the lives of far too many people. Coming to grips with difficult and uninviting, painful circumstances, ranks high on my list of struggles in life.

My observations of, and conversations with, Ron and Lib helped me better understand and address my tendency to struggle through the difficult times while not dealing with the causes and negative impact of unacceptable conditions and circumstances. They have had, and continue to experience, this need to come to grips. Because their journey in this area has helped me so much, some of their own "coming to grips" experiences are shared in this chapter.

Ron's attitude, for many years, regarding the celebration of his birthday is a good starting point for showing how coming to grips looks in action. Even though Lib and the children would prepare a birthday celebration for him and they were happy and excited to do so, he approached these celebrations with obvious dread and a lack of excitement.

Unknowingly, Ron would do things in an attempt to discourage Lib from arranging a celebration of his birthday. Then came a time when he was approaching a birthday in the 45-50 year range. On this occasion, he had done something of that discouraging nature and then slipped away to a place in the house where he could be alone. Ron says Lib found him and, without notice, said, "I am sick and tired of you behaving this way as your birthday nears. You make a special effort to do something to make me mad at you and I want you to stop behaving that way."

Ron explains that Lib's words made him realize what he was doing. His response was to not only recognize what he was doing and correct it, but acknowledge that it was unacceptable and to unpack why he was doing it. The "why" required, with God's leading, honest self-examination. It was all about the death of his mother. In his words:

> ***"She died in the hospital three weeks after giving birth to her seventh child. She was buried on my eighth birthday. Her death and then her funeral on my birthday blocks out virtually all memories prior to that event. Birthdays were always sad times for me and I grew up thinking I should not be happy on my birthday because being happy would mean that I didn't care that my mother had died. Unknowingly, I would do things to make Lib not want to do anything special for my birthday."***

Ron recognized what was true regarding his mother's death and, as a result, was able to eliminate mistaken ideas. Another essential element in Ron's processing was that he heard Lib's words, but also recognized her love and pain. Since that coming to grips moment, Ron and the family have been able to happily celebrate his birthday.

Here is a brief detour that demonstrates how Ron and Lib's story can positively influence other relationships. I started writing the first draft of this chapter during the very early morning of 29 March 2024. About mid-morning, my wife, Denise, and I started a walk along our regular route in the neighborhood. I was in a good mood. We were walking and talking. Then she asked if it was "okay" to hold my hand. In responding, instead of simply saying "yes", I asked why she felt the need to ask. I did not simply ask why, but did so in a manner that caused her to go silent. I did not see where the silence was justified. My response was to, in frustration with myself, give the walk up and head home as Denise called out to me.

Thankfully, as I pushed the remote and waited for the garage door to go up, God reminded me of what I had written about Ron and Lib just a few hours earlier. I turned to go back and make things right with Denise. As I turned, she was approaching our home. I walked out to her and, with profound remorse, apologized for what I had done by way of abruptly going home. I requested that we continue the walk and talk about what had happened. At first, she hesitated to agree that we continue the walk. Without giving details of what I had written, I explained that reflecting on an experience shared with me by Ron and Lib, I quickly realized that my choice to go home was wrong.

We continued the walk and reconciled; quickly moved beyond what, although seemingly minor, could have been very disruptive in our relationship. As minor as this example might seem, it illustrates how I hope, even pray, that Ron and Lib's story will give birth to this kind of experience in many other relationships.

Now, continuing with Ron and Lib on coming to grips. Lib shares an experience that fits here. She had an older sister who, in

Lib's view, was their father's favorite. When that sister was eight years old and Lib was six, Lib had made some chocolate milk by mixing chocolate with regular milk. She went to the bathroom and, upon returning to the kitchen, discovered that her sister had drunk her chocolate milk.

Lib was very angry. Given that the family had a cow and the refrigerator held ample milk, all her sister had to do was pour some milk and add chocolate to her own cup. Instead, she, by Lib's definition, "stole" Lib's milk. Lib had long fingernails and, in her anger, scratched her sister. While taking no action regarding the older daughter having "stolen" the milk, her father cut Lib's fingernails to the nub as punishment for scratching her sister. Given that her father took no action toward the older sister for "stealing" Lib's milk, Lib was extremely upset and did not speak to her father for three weeks. As she shares this experience all these years later, there still seems to be a tinge of disappointment and anger.

However, in sharing that experience, Lib gives information that indicates she has done some coming to grips with the experience. First, her sister had what was referred to as a "leaking heart". This was probably a "leaky heart valve" where one of the four valves in the heart does not close tightly. Given this medical condition, her sister probably needed the extra special attention Lib perceived was being given by her parents. Second, she was the firstborn child.

As Lib reflects on these two points, it is obvious that she sees the situation for what it was and is dealing with it forthrightly. There is no wallowing in a world of imagination, but simply, with clear-headed reasoning, examining the facts and responding accordingly. That is, she was not in a position to change the circumstances and, also, given her sister's medical condition, was able to see the situation from her father's perspective. Lib could not bring about a change in how her father seemed to favor her sister. The three weeks of not speaking to him did not produce a better situation.

However, Ron shares an experience where, as in the opening account in this chapter, he came to grips in a fashion that allowed him to address and move through a time of fear.

This happened when, primarily because of Ron encouraging her to do so, Lib started college. Ron says that Lib starting college was a "difficult time" for him. She had been a stay-at-home wife and mother for some 13 years. His job situation allowed him to stop by home and have lunch; he knew Lib would be there. With the start of this college adventure, he says his "old mind" started thinking, "Ron, you gonna lose her now." With laughter - and saying he is joking - Ron states that he was afraid she would run off with some younger professor.

In this particular circumstance, Ron did not raise his concern with Lib and, without any foundation, imply lack of trust in her love for and commitment to him. Instead, he came to grips with what was happening in him. Elsewhere, Ron shares that they had gotten into a married-life routine. Against that backdrop, given this new concern on his part, he determined that he would be more attentive to Lib, and that is what he did. With that decision, and following through, he was able to be comfortable with, and very supportive of, Lib's college endeavor.

How a person deals with coming to grips is greatly impacted by the experiences across the length and breadth of our living. Not only must we consider this truth as we confront challenges in one's own life, but also in the lives of others with whom we are in relationship. Ron and Lib's accounts regarding Ron's father illustrate this point.

Ron describes his father as being "tough and thick-skinned, ruler of his house, with tremendous drive, uneven in when he disciplined children". Lib adds that Ron's father thought that Ron was "henpecked". She goes on to say that Ron was not "the king in the house" and she never felt like she needed to "kowtow" or bow down to him. She says further, "Ron's dad wasn't sure that was the way a man ought to treat his wife. She ought to be under his thumb all the time. Ronald didn't want me to be under his thumb; he wanted me to be by his side."

Many people, faced with a father who presented himself as Ron's father is described in that preceding paragraph, would separate from him and never look back. That was not Ron's response. Instead, with grace and mercy as his guide, Ron sought to understand how his father came to be as he was; to respond to him with due consideration of that history.

Here is some of that history as Ron, with obvious love for and understanding of his father, shared it. Ron's father's father died when his father was 15 years old and left his mother with seven children to rear. The mother never remarried. Consequently, Ron's father grew up without a father-image. Born in 1899, he went on to accomplish a milestone that was rare in that time; he graduated from high school.

After a move to Michigan, where he worked as a telegrapher with the railroad, Ron's father met and married a young lady who had been an orphan. They had a son and, a couple of years later, she gave birth to a daughter. The daughter died six months after her birth and the mother died six months after her daughter's death. Ron's father said she died of "heart break". Here his father was - a single parent in his mid-20s.

Later, this young father met and married the lady who would become Ron's mother. She gave birth to seven children in 12 years. After the birth of the seventh child, she never came home from the hospital; she died. His father, who was a month shy of age 40, was left to rear eight children. This was in October of 1939.

In July of 1940, his father married Ron's stepmother. With obvious joy and thanksgiving, Ron says this was the best thing for his father at that time. They were married for 40 years, until his father's death. In later chapters, there is more detail regarding Ron's mother and stepmother. Here, suffice it to say, his mother and stepmother impacted Ron's life in amazingly positive ways.

In 1940, the family moved from Indianapolis, Indiana to Fayetteville, North Carolina where his father worked at Fort Bragg as Post Engineer. He continued in that job until retirement.

Ron's stepmother made it clear that she would discipline the young children but not the older ones; that would be left to their father. Ron says his father's discipline was uneven. For instance, there were times when he and the other older children would be punished if not home at a certain time; on other occasions, nothing would be said. Consequently, he grew up thinking, "I don't know what's right and what's wrong."

Ron is able to look at all of this and more, then say with obvious deep feeling, "Dad lived a hard life; worked hard for everything he got." Being able to sort through and come to grips with the circumstances of his father's life allowed him to still build a positive and productive relationship. This process was helped by Ron's capacity for giving appropriate attention to what might seem like minor events. When Ron joined the Society of Engineers, his father joined. When he joined a Masonic Lodge, his father joined a year or so later. When Ron became pastor of Lake Lynn Baptist Church, although his father was a member of a Presbyterian church, he would, from time-to-time, worship at Lake Lynn and showed tremendous approval of what Ron was about in his life and in service to God and God's people. With total confidence, Ron says, "I knew my father loved me."

Maybe the lesson from Ron's experience with his father is that coming to grips with our stuff might also require coming to grips with the stuff of other folk.

The final piece for this chapter points up the need for individuals to come to grips with one's basic makeup and, with God's help coupled with the boundaries provided by Him, live in accordance with that makeup. The accompanying challenge is to allow others to follow this process in their living and not pressure them to be like us.

This matter of being comfortable in who one is, and allowing others to do the same, shows through in Ron and Lib dealing with one of them being an introvert and the other an extrovert. Lib is the extrovert and, given that Ron is an introvert, they had to work through the difficulties caused by this fact of life. Lib shares that early in their marriage, and for several years, she was at home caring for children. Further, they lived in an area distant from other people; there was nobody for her to talk with. Ron was at work all day and interacting with people. He would come home tired and simply want to rest. Consequently, for the most part, her missing interaction with others was made even weightier.

On the other hand, especially as the years passed, Ron was able to recognize Lib's extroversion and, early on, found it hard to accept. In fact he admits being "jealous" of her extroversion.

Then came Ron being considered for a job with the Home Mission Board of the Southern Baptist Convention. Part of the screening process was for Ron and Lib to be interviewed by a psychiatrist. He administered the Myers-Briggs Personality Test. The tests clearly showed Ron to be introverted and Lib as extroverted.

Ron was troubled by his results because he saw his result as failure and he was one who had excelled time and again. Ron explains that test results were presented in a graph with a horizontal line across the middle of it. Lib's line was high above that horizontal line, indicating her strong extroversion. Ron's line was below the horizontal line, moving toward it and then away. He was introverted, less at times than others. Ron talked with the psychiatrist about his results. The response was that his results did not show him to be a failure. Instead, they did show him to be introverted, but able to function in an extroverted mode under circumstances where he is comfortable. Ron understood this explanation and was able to accept his introversion.

In fact, during a discussion of a religious topic while teaching at The University of North Carolina at Pembroke, Ron shared his understanding of his introversion. He explained to the class that, given his introversion, it would not seem possible for him to teach a class of 45 students and be comfortable doing so; being in his comfort zone made it possible.

That Myers-Briggs experience opened Ron and Lib's eyes to what they were facing in this extrovert/introvert fact-of-life. Instead of moving on as usual, they gave attention to the hand they were dealt. Again, they came to grips with what was real. Lib accepted Ron's introversion; even realizing his need for time alone, for "me time". Ron recognized Lib's acceptance of his introversion and this recognition, coupled with his newly found understanding of their situation, accepted Lib's extroversion. They have not; do not try to change one another.

A final thought on coming to grips has to do with how doing so, or not doing so, affects one's relationship with God and the fruit of that relationship in a person's life. Without doubt, Ron and Lib Loftis have the peace and joy that a close walk with God promises to provide. They have it not only because of faith in God and commitment to His way, but because that relationship is coupled with attention to emotional health; part of which is coming to grips. Peter Scazzero puts it this way in his book, Emotionally Healthy Spirituality:

"Christian spirituality, without an integration of emotional health, can be deadly-to yourself, your relationship with God, and the people around you. I know. Having lived half my adult life this way, I have more personal illustrations than I care to recount." [2]

CHAPTER FIVE

THE BIGGER PICTURE OF BUILDING A "STRONG FAMILY"

"Strong families help children feel safe and secure. Strong families have warmth and care, good communication, predictability, and strong connections to others outside the family."[1]

Without doubt, Ron and Lib built a strong family with their children and the generations beyond those children. The truth of that statement is reflected throughout their journey together. By no means would they claim perfection in their immediate family. However, without reservation, I state that they built, and continue to maintain, a strong family.

This chapter does not address the inner-workings of their immediate household. Rather, the aim here is to provide a feel for some of the life experiences that must have influenced how they went about being family in their home and across all the years of their marriage; even to this day. This means looking all the way back to their youth. As with every part of this book, the hope is that readers will find bits of truth that help them along the way to building a successful marriage. The fact of life is that family relationships and experiences, internal and external to a home, affect a marriage.

Ron's mother died when he was eight years old. His mother loved him and he knew that to be true. However, she gave birth to seven children in 12 years. A young daughter had some developmental delay issues. This daughter's condition, along with caring for all of the other children, made it difficult for her to give each child the attention she clearly desired to give. Her death came three weeks after giving birth to Paul David.

After Ron's mother's death, her mother strongly pressed his father to "farm" the children out to relatives. In even stronger terms, he refused to even consider separating his children from himself and one another.

About six months after Ron's mother's death, his father married Margaret Hazalet Tingle. She had two older daughters, one of whom was married. She made it clear to the children that she would be closely parenting the three youngest children, but time proved that she loved and cared for them all. She said if the three youngest wanted to call her "Ma", that was fine; but only if they wanted to do so. The others were to call her "Margaret". Ron says, "She became the mother of all of the children; she might as well have given birth to our baby brother." When Ron was 10 years old, the family moved to Fayetteville, North Carolina. His stepmother focused on rearing children and taking care of the home. Although she had worked at a grocery store in Indianapolis, she never worked outside the home after marrying Ron's father.

Ron's love and appreciation for his stepmother showed through on many occasions and in many ways. One of those was when he preached in a homecoming service at Big Rock Presbyterian Church in Hope Mills, North Carolina, where his father and stepmother had been members. In his sermon, Ron mentioned his stepmother.

Two to three years later, he was working at Pinecrest Funeral Home. A lady from the church where he had preached those years before saw him and said, "Ronald, I did not know that Margaret was not your birthmother until you mentioned it that Sunday." About that experience, and that lady's comment, Ron says, "That one statement tells the whole story of my stepmother." He goes on to say, "Every one of our children loved my stepmother like I did. Our spouses loved her like we did." As Ron makes these comments, Lib wholeheartedly agrees. Ron's stepmother was in his life from age 10 to 51. Forty-one years after her death, as he speaks, his love and appreciation for her shines like the sun on a clear day.

Among Ron's siblings, loving his stepmother was, by no means, limited to Ron. His brother Paul David, the youngest child, lived in Indianapolis, Indiana as an adult. When Margaret's health failed, Paul David would, with his family, drive to Hope Mills to visit his stepmother. His wife would clean the house thoroughly from front to back, top to bottom. Paul David made these trips even though his finances were limited. Their sister, Marilyn, who lived in the Hope Mills area, was faithful in caring for Margaret.

Then there was Ron's oldest sibling, a half-brother, who was, as Ron states it, "...virtually a grown man when their father married their stepmother." However, she was a mother even to him. That brother was drafted into the U.S. Army during World War II and participated in one of the Normandy (France) landings. His father did not hear from that son for one year. Then he received a 15 page letter from him saying that all was well. This was a time of great relief for their father and the family.

As much love as there was in the Loftis family, the family was not without challenges. Ron's father's view on interactions between people often challenged the goal of being a happy, loving family. Ron's assessment is that his father thought Ron was "henpecked". He felt that his son should take charge; not give in to Lib.

At Christmas time one year, the family was together and Margaret, Ron's stepmother, wanted pecan pies, but did not like making them. Lib volunteered to make the pies. Margaret explained that she had picked out the pecans and wanted to know if anything else was needed. Lib responded by saying, "No, but if anything else is needed, I will send Ron to the store." Her father-in-law heard the exchange and, in an angry tone, said, "I'll be 'd' if you would send me anywhere. I might go if you asked me." Ron assesses this exchange as happening because he and his father were very close and his father might have seen Lib as a threat to that relationship. The cooking went on.

Against the backdrop of the pie-cooking episode, consider these comments from Lib regarding her father-in-law:

> ***"Let me tell you one thing about my father-in-law so you won't think I despised him; I really didn't. I admired him tremendously. When Ron's stepmother became an invalid, he took care of her like she might have been his baby. Very protective, very protective. And he learned to do things and did them that he wouldn't have done earlier. He cooked for her and cleaned her and cleaned house. And all of the things that were not common for him as a younger man. One thing for sure; she did not lack for anything. That was impressive."***

As Ron and Lib share the demanding and difficult experiences that they, and others, had with his father, he makes it crystal clear that he loved and respected his father. As indicated in chapter four and elsewhere in this book, they had a close and lasting relationship.

Lib allowed me to read a paper that she titled "Grandma's Memories of Childhood". In it, she recounts experiences from her growing-up years. The memories run from her father working in a textile mill, but having to leave that job due to the impact on his body, to playing with her siblings and cousins, sustaining a broken arm, helping in growing and canning vegetables, the harsh effects of World War II, frequent moves from one house to another, and improved living conditions. She describes the conditions in one house as follows:

> ***"We moved into an old storage house. It was one big room - beds on one end; kitchen on the other!... We moved into three of the five rooms - no floor in the other two. Daddy worked to get those done and put doors in place. Glad it was summer! As long as we lived there it was never finished. We did have a bedroom for Mom and Dad and a bedroom for the four children. There was a kitchen, dining room and living room-plus the back porch that was screened in."***

Then there is this very relevant account that she shared with me in conversation regarding her mother:

> ***"Mama told stories about her childhood. She only had a mother, an aged grandmother, an aunt, and a cousin. She remembered going to her father's grave with her mother, Bell, when she was very small. They had been told that he died during the First World War. I'm not sure where they lived, maybe Columbus County, NC..... Daddy lived on a nearby farm. When another man her mother's age wanted to go out with my mother, whose name was Daisy, she refused. So he 'courted' my mother's mother, Bell, and eventually married her. My mother was told the man bragged that he would "marry the mother and get the daughter, too". Even though my grandmother married the man***

> ***and moved from living with her family members, my mother refused to live with them and continued living with her grandmother, an aunt, and cousin. She quit school when she was 14 years old and went to work in the cotton mill to support herself while continuing to live with her grandmother, aunt, and cousin. It was then that she and Daddy decided to marry. She was 15; he was 16. Any wonder that she felt getting married was the right thing to do? She worked six days a week, 12 hours a day. Daddy and farming probably sounded like paradise. They were married August 17, 1929. Just two months later, the stock market crashed and the Great Depression began."***

The aim in sharing the accounts reflected in this chapter is to contend that these kinds of experiences reflect some keys to building strong families; recognizing that family members, internal and external to a home, impact a marriage. Among these keys are the following:

1. Do not give up in the face of loss and difficulty. This shows through in Ron's father refusing to distribute his children among relatives after the death of his wife and the family moving on to successful relationships with Ron's stepmother.
2. Be reasonable and rational in setting boundaries for relationships. Ron's stepmother did this in determining and executing her role in rearing Ron and his siblings.
3. As Ron and his siblings did toward their stepmother, even in changing and difficult times: appreciate being loved.
4. As demonstrated in Lib's experience with moving from house to house and being affected by her father's job change: stay the course to overcoming.

5. Like Lib's mother when approached by a man who wanted to date her: be clear-headed in assessing possible relationships and other decisions.
6. As Ron and Lib did with Ron's father: assess people in their totality. That is, look at the whole picture and not just the negatives in a person's conduct and presence. Consider what factors have shaped a person and give fair attention to the likelihood of future improved behavior.

The list above is not all-inclusive, but is intended to give a sense of the kinds of experiences and influences that impacted how Ron and Lib went about successfully being family in their immediate household; and, thereby, successful in their marriage. Be advised, there is nothing automatic about following even the six conditions above. Ron and Lib's journey shows that it requires commitment to the process and a close relationship with God.

Given that there is no mention of God or faith in this chapter, one might wonder why the "close relationship with God" reference is in the preceding paragraph. It is because, in every aspect of their living, Ron and Lib Loftis have and continue to make relationship with God their first priority. Everything else, including how they dealt with and continue to address being family, is done in light of their relationship with God and His direction for their living.

CHAPTER SIX

REARING AND BEING BLESSED BY CHILDREN

"The Adequate Family and the Optimal Family: In these families there is an ability to be flexible and cherish each individual member while at the same time valuing a sense of closeness. Good feelings, trust, and teamwork by the parents enable members to work through difficulties and conflicts. What distinguishes level Two families from level One can be summed up in one word: delight. Level One families truly delight in being with one another."[1]

The quote above addresses two of the five ways of looking at and understanding families. Level Two is described in the first part of that quote. Moving from Level Two to Level One requires that, in addition to the Level Two elements, a family "delight in being with one another". Level One is the standard that every family should aim to achieve. As I consider all the years of my life, I am not able to identify a single family that might fit the Level One description. Maybe there were Level Twos. The caveat is that I have not been in a position to closely observe a large number of families.

However, I have very closely observed the family of Ron and Lib Loftis. Without reservation, and with total confidence, I state that this is a Level One family. This chapter, in particular, paints a verbal picture that supports that conclusion. Further, as with every chapter in this book, the hope is that the accounts here will prove helpful for others who desire to have their family achieve Level One or even simply move closer to it.

One might wonder why the state of a family, even beyond those family members who live in a household, would be considered in a discussion of achieving a successful marriage. Let the record be clear: the interactions and quality of relationships between family members, even external to a home, affect marriages. For instance, if a child has behavior problems or academic difficulty, his or her parents' marriage will be affected.

The elements considered here are in no particular order. Let's start with the fact that Lib was a stay-at-home mother for 13 years. In our time, 2024, this arrangement is not held in high esteem. There are articles galore that address that truth. Given the positive outcomes of this family, one might want to consider the extent to which Lib's time at home with children positively impacted the still ongoing unitedness of this family.

Among many, an article by Nikkya Hargrove titled "It's Time to Finally Ditch the Stigma Against Stay-at-Home Moms" forthrightly addresses this issue. Here is the thinking of one mother as reflected in the article:

> *"Sarah King, a 33-year-old mom of two who lives in Stamford, Connecticut, says, 'I chose to stay home. We've always been a single-income family. It's something I take a great deal of strength and inspiration from. I wanted to raise really good humans and to establish a relationship with them, which takes both time and patience.'"*[2]

All those years ago, Ron and Lib understood what the mother quoted above believes and is experiencing. There may be cases where mothers cannot stay at home with children due to financial considerations or other factors. Again, Ron and Lib's experience indicates, where possible, that this is a key ingredient for building a Level One family.

After being at home for years caring for children, Lib started and finished college. During that time, the children picked up some of the household chores. They cleaned and even, at times, made dinner and had it ready on time. They took on other tasks that fit with their capabilities. They were taught to do their laundry and did it.

Regarding doing laundry, Lib shares that there was an incident where she had a bright yellow dress. The children put it in the washing machine with some new blue jeans that had never been washed. That dress came out blue. Lib admits being upset. However, she decided that it could not make things worse if she put it in the washing machine with a lot of bleach. She did so and the dress came out perfectly yellow again.

The family's support of Ron's call to ministry is another area for consideration. My observation of American society in 2024 is that husbands and wives, along with other members of a household, in most instances, focus on individual endeavors. That is, the normal approach is for the husband and wife to each have wage-earning employment that is a primary focus for each of them. That makes what happens in the home, in the family, secondary or even less in importance. That was not the case with this family. Ron's ministry was central and even though she taught school in later years, Lib treated Ron's calling as the primary focus between their two careers.

I am sure that some will read that preceding paragraph and conclude that the case being made is that a husband's career should always have a family's primary focus. That is not the point. The point is that between a husband and wife as parents, the best arrangement seems to be that a family focuses on the career of one parent, even if both are working. My opinion is that, and I own it as my opinion, in a two-parent household with children, one parent's primary responsibility must be providing financially while the other must have greater flexibility to deal with children - even if he or she works. That means the primary breadwinner may be the husband or wife. In fact, Ron and Lib have a son who works, but is the primary caregiver for the children as his wife works in a financially rewarding, but demanding, profession.

Ron and Lib made it a high priority to introduce their children to the importance of education. Given my observations of them, I am sure that they did not use a force-feeding approach. Instead, they reasoned with their children and led by example. They did instill that a twelfth-grade education would not be sufficient; the goal should be at least an undergraduate college degree. Without doubt, making education a high priority contributed, and continues to contribute, to the success and closeness of this family; even down through generations beyond Ron and Lib's children.

Here is another indicator of the soundness of this family. All of their children and grandchildren are self-sufficient. None of them has ever been a financial drain on Ron and Lib. Further, not one of them has ever been in legal trouble. Those are telling statements regarding this family.

I found it worthy of attention when Ron and Lib explained that they go to bed together at the same time every night. One might read in the bed and the other goes to sleep, but they are there together. Ron admits that if he awakens during the night, he might get up and do work on his computer. By that point, Lib is asleep.

All the way back to my teenage years, I have been one who works best late at night and into the early morning. Most nights, my wife is in the bed at 9:00 PM and up at 5:00 AM. Across the years, she has asked me to, a couple of nights each week, go to bed when she does. I tried it, but not with any real commitment. However, when Ron and Lib told me about their practice, I started working on going to bed at the same time as my wife on a far more frequent basis. I am making progress and, even though it might seem minor, I see value in making it happen.

Then, all the way back to when Lib was teaching in local schools, Ron would make coffee for her. After all these years, he still makes coffee for her.

At this juncture, a reasonable question is "What's the point?" My aim is to share some actions and decisions that helped make and sustain this Level One family. Then, the closeness and cooperative spirit of the family heighten the joy and unity in Ron and Lib's marriage. One only has to hear them talk about how their children and grandchildren insist on caring for them. Their reporting is not done with any hint of bragging. It is about pure thanksgiving for the love and concern that is reflected in actions toward them.

For instance, Ron was hospitalized and about to come home. Ronald Jr. was in town awaiting Ron's release. He simply announced that he and his siblings were going to purchase a lift chair for Ron. With Lib, he went to a furniture store, selected a chair, and had it delivered.

The children have done the same thing by way of arranging for lawn care and the cleaning of Ron and Lib's home. The lady, Carol, who does the cleaning, has become a real friend to Lib. They make runs to Hamrick's, a store that Lib loves. Ron and Lib have no idea how much these services cost; their children simply make them happen and pay the bills.

Allow a detour here for a "God moment". Debbie, their son Ron's wife, found Carol. She had previously operated a cleaning business, but had closed it long before being contacted by Debbie. Carol also thought that any online presence had been discontinued. Despite all of this, Debbie found Carol online and contacted her.

As might be expected, Ron and Lib were concerned about the cost of what was being done for them. When Ron raised the concern, Ronald Jr. responded, "Consider it this way. Divide the price that you would have to pay by four. Each one of us pays a fourth." After sharing that exchange, Ron said, "One kid might stand by parents, but four?"

Even beyond arranging for others to do work, Michael and his wife come down and work on Ron and Lib's home; among many actions are a landing in the garage and safety features in the bathrooms.

Ron makes great use of his computer. Among other things, he sends out prayer requests to a group of prayer partners. His computer was working sporadically. After Ron had gone through a short period of repair efforts, the children announced to him that a new computer was being purchased, delivered, and set up.

This is not a case of children and grandchildren supporting from a distance while not having time together. Here is just one of many indicators of this family's togetherness. In July 2023, there was a family gathering at the Loftis' home in Hope Mills, North Carolina. Including Ron and Lib, there were 30 family members. This was a weekend event. On Sunday morning, Ron and Lib headed off to Sunday school and worship without asking any of the other family members to come to worship. Without being asked, 19 of the 28 visiting family members showed up for worship. Be reminded that, in a single-family home, they had to shower, prepare and eat breakfast, then make the trip to First Baptist Church in Fayetteville. This was about faith and family.

Here is another indicator of this family's commitment to God's way. Steve, the third son, was pastoring a church in Hobbsville, North Carolina. He met and was prepared to marry Lee, who was working in nearby Elizabeth City. Before they had married, the opportunity for a family trip came along. Debbie, a daughter-in-law, was invited to sing for a wedding that took place on a cruise ship while in port before starting a cruise. Debbie commented that she wished she could have stayed for the cruise.

Since Ron and Lib were about to celebrate their 50th wedding anniversary, Lib said, "We'll just spend your inheritance and take you on a cruise for our 50th wedding anniversary." They were getting ready for this trip in 2002.

Steve and Lee were not married and somebody asked Lee if she was going. Steve and Lee had a room, but Lib said, "We must have a wedding before we go on a cruise." Lee said, "I just need somebody to come and help me." Lib responded, "Would you like for me to come spend a week with you and we will get this wedding going?" Lee said, "Yes." Lib went to Elizabeth City, North Carolina, and stayed with Lee in her apartment. The wedding was planned and carried out. Ron officiated. After a honeymoon, Steve and Lee went on the cruise as husband and wife. This was being faithful to God's way.

There is an extremely critical piece that is absolutely required for building and nurturing a Level One family or coming close to doing so. Lib shared a statement that appears in various forms, but I could not find it exactly as she stated it: "The most important thing that parents can give their children is for the children to know that their parents love each other."

So, there it is; marriages that have the presence of joy and unity, that are successful, do not happen in a vacuum. My experiences and observations say that one of the primary influences on every marriage is family in the home and external to it. Not an exhaustive list, but some pointers from Ron and Lib's past and ongoing experience of family positively impacting their marriage follow:

1. Make it a goal to build a family that delights in being with one another.

2. Where children are involved, ensure that one parent has primary responsibility for the day-to-day care of those children while the other is primarily responsible for financial support of the household.
3. Share household tasks among all members of the immediate family.
4. Between husband and wife, give attention to what might seem like simple actions (shared bedtime, coffee for a spouse). Not only does this positively affect the marital relationship, but it signals, to children, the love between parents.
5. As a family, be understanding and supportive of the work situations of husbands and wives, mothers and fathers. This is especially important when demanding careers are involved.
6. By way of education and other actions, guide children in preparing for independent living as adults.
7. Do not make demands for financial or other support from children, but when it is provided, be cooperative and thankful.
8. As parents, live before children in such a way that they know their mother and father love each other.
9. Know and live by God's standards while being sure to teach them to your children. Do not hesitate to call on your children to live by those standards.

CHAPTER SEVEN

EDUCATION AS A HIGH PRIORITY

"It's not just the diploma: education is important in building knowledge and developing literacy, thinking and problem-solving skills, and character traits."[1]

Given that the purpose of this book is to provide some considerations relating to building a successful marriage, one might wonder why there would be mention of the importance of educating children. It is here because my experiences and observations of others make it crystal clear that having children definitely presents some challenges in a marriage. Beyond what happens during the growing-up years, even greater complications and marital stress are likely in later years where children are not, when younger, provided the support and direction that contribute to sound preparation for becoming balanced and self-supporting adults. The resulting actions of those adult children can disrupt their parents' marriage beyond description.

Let the record be clear, I am not alone in contending that having children can lead to stress in a marriage. In an article titled "Coping With the Stress Children Add to a Marriage", Elizabeth Scott, PhD, addresses this fact of life:

"Sometimes the addition of kids can lead to marriage problems you may not have expected. It's a common experience: You had a wonderfully romantic relationship—then you add kids to the mix and everything's a little more stressful, less romantic, and less satisfying.

Some of the problems that couples face after having children include:

- ***Conflicts over parenting***
- ***Difficulty spending time with one another***
- ***Fatigue and lack of sleep***
- ***Financial challenges***
- ***Intimacy issues***
- ***Lack of support***
- ***No alone time***
- ***Stress caused by trying to juggle kids, work, relationships, and other obligations"***[2]

My observation is that Ron and Lib understood the importance of education in preparing their children for successful independent living as adults. Further, it does not appear that they factored in how their emphasis on educating their children, along with other actions, would help them avoid most, if not all, of the problems listed above. Where any of those problems did arise, they were successfully dealt with quickly and in a loving fashion. Although I do not see any indication that Ron and Lib focused on the education of their children as a factor in strengthening their marriage; the marriage was positively affected. Consequently, parents would do well, early on, to consider Ron and Lib's focus on education and the impact of it regarding their children and their marriage.

From early in their marriage, Ron and Lib determined that they would aim to have all four of their children get a college education. As I write this chapter in June 2024, all four of the Loftis children have college degrees, seven of the nine grandchildren have earned degrees, the eighth grandchild started college in the fall of 2023, and the ninth is an excellent high school student who will definitely enter college in the fall of 2025. That is the big picture of what this family has done by way of education. What follows in this chapter is greater detail as to how they did it and a wider picture of specific accomplishments. Again, all of this is presented to show the probable positive impact of education in building successful marriages. It should be noted that this attention to education not only positively impacted Ron and Lib's marriage, but did the same in the marriages of their descendants.

An essential element in the Loftis education plan was for the four children to understand that 12 years of education would not be sufficient; they should plan on at least an undergraduate college degree. Every indication is that the children understood and fully embraced this thinking. That was done when 12 years of education was generally seen as sufficient.

The other element that must have influenced those children's commitment to education as a high priority was seeing both their parents work toward degrees. Ron and Lib were in college at a time when the children were old enough to be aware of those endeavors. They experienced the power of example.

Then, Ron and Lib started early in planning financially for the education of their children. This is a critical piece that is missed by far too many families. My observation is that families get so caught up in the present by way of keeping children engaged in various activities that they do not prepare for those college years. The result is that when the time for college comes, there is a financial scramble as to how the college costs will be paid. For many parents and children, the result is the financial strain of loans, along with the mental and emotional distress that often follows. I suggest that even if a child goes to college, this lack of financial preparation on the part of parents will very likely strain the parents' marriage. As stated in an earlier chapter, when the four children finished their undergraduate degrees, there was not a single loan outstanding for Ron, Lib, or any of the children. All bills were paid.

Be reminded that Ron resigned from a well-paying job with the State of North Carolina in order to accept God's call of him to ministry. That action came with a substantial reduction in financial income just as the oldest child was entering college. Ron and Lib make it clear that the family's educational accomplishments in the face of reduced income are viewed as God's confirmation of Ron's call to ministry.

Now, let's move on to greater detail regarding this family's education journey. The greater detail is important because it helps one understand how a family might work together in this process and the reasonably expected positive impact on a family; consequently, on a marriage.

Michael (Mike), the second oldest child, is a good starting point for addressing this family's education journey. Mike started his college career at North Carolina State University. Ron says Mike majored in watching basketball, swimming, etc. This went on to the point that he was advised to "Go home and grow up". Mike came home. He spent some time working at Miller and Rhodes Department Store selling ladies' shoes. However, he did not stay there and wallow in his circumstance.

Instead, he and his older brother, Ronald Jr., met their wives in the singles program at Knollwood Baptist Church in Winston-Salem. When Mike and his wife-to-be, Ann, started considering marriage, she encouraged him to go back to college. Ann explained that since she was working as a teacher, she would cover expenses so that Mike could attend college. They got married and followed that plan.

Mike enrolled at the University of North Carolina at Charlotte and earned a degree in civil engineering. Over the years that followed, he worked with Lowes Companies, Inc. supervising the building of stores in the northeast section of the United State. After years in that job, his positon was eliminated and Mike left the company with financial security.

Allow me a brief comment regarding Mike's story. When he came home from North Carolina State University, he could have, as is often the case in our time, lounged around at his parents' house. In so doing, he would have, most likely, caused some stress in his parents' marriage. Instead, he found a job, got on his financial feet, and quickly moved on to even better employment in Winston-Salem. That move led to marriage and a very successful work-life.

A bit of repetition here. Having spent substantial time observing and talking with Ron and Lib, I am totally convinced that their planning for and encouraging college education for their children was because of their concern that those children be prepared for success in life. I have seen no indication that they considered the possible negative impact on their marriage if any one of those children, as an adult, had to live with them long-term. However, without reservation, I contend that parents better consider that failing to prepare children for independent living as adults will very likely negatively impact those parents' relationship at some point; even as that failure is taking place during the early years of a child's life. The education piece is just one consideration in preparing children for independent living as adults. Education is given substantial attention here because Ron and Lib did it for their children and did it so well.

Looking beyond Mike's education experience and achievements, Ron and Lib's success in developing and executing a plan for ensuring that each of their children earned at least a bachelor's degree can be tremendously informative for other parents. For that reason, what follows is a look at the education journeys of the other three children; Ron Jr., Steve, and Lisa.

Ron Jr. was a good student in high school. He was editor of the high school yearbook. The yearbook staff took a trip to Winston-Salem to meet with the yearbook publisher. Ron asked if the group could visit Wake Forest University. They were allowed to visit. Lib says, "Ron Jr. came home 'alive'." He was a Morehead Scholar and, therefore, applied for the Morehead Scholarship that was only available at the University of North Carolina at Chapel Hill. Not being selected for that scholarship was a bit of a letdown for Ron Jr. However, the visit to Wake Forest produced a turnaround. He was excited and told Lib he had to go to Wake Forest.

Ron Jr. applied to Wake Forest and was accepted. He received the George Foster Hankins Scholarship and it paid a substantial portion of his college expenses. Again, this was another case of God answering prayer. Ron Jr. enjoyed his undergraduate experience and did well at Wake Forest. One year, he was editor of the yearbook. At his own expense, Ron Jr. went on to earn an MBA (Master of Business Administration).

Lib and Ron believe that by the time Steve, their third child, went to college, he was feeling a call to ministry. He chose to attend Wake Forest University. He stayed on campus and did well. After being in school for a while, he declared his major as religion. Steve told Ron that he tried to talk with every department head and the only one who would give him any time was the Religion Department Head. Steve saw this as God saying that he should major in religion.

When Steve finished at Wake Forest University, he went on to earn a Master of Divinity (MDiv) at Southeastern Baptist Theological Seminary in Wake Forest, North Carolina. Steve pastored several churches in North Carolina and earned a Doctor of Ministry (DMin) at Baptist Theological Seminary of Richmond in Richmond, Virginia.

Lisa, the youngest child, earned her undergraduate degree from Meredith College in Raleigh, North Carolina. Lisa's course to Meredith highlights Ron and Lib's commitment to their children's education. Lisa was part of a group of girls who were invited to visit the college. Lib was teaching and couldn't get away to make the trip with Lisa. Consequently, Ron went with her to Raleigh to spend the day at Meredith.

She did the day-long tour. At the end of the day, Lisa said to Ron, "This is where I want to go to college." Ron responded, "OK, let's see what we can do." All went extremely well and Lisa earned her four year degree. Over time, she also earned a master's degree in Middle School Education and another in Counseling. Across the years, she was a classroom teacher and then a school counselor.

To this point in the chapter, the focus has been on Ron and Lib making education a major point of emphasis in preparing their children for independent living as adults. It is obvious that they talked with their children about the importance of getting an education. However, in my estimation, the power and the effectiveness of modeling what we call others to is far greater than mere words. Ron and Lib's education endeavors are mentioned in previous chapters. However, greater detail is appropriate here in emphasizing the need for and the power of modeling what is desired of children.

Consider Lib's college process. She and Ron got married two weeks after Lib's nineteenth birthday. After having been a stay-at-home wife and mother for 13 years, she entered college at the University of North Carolina at Pembroke. Chapter Three recounts Ron encouraging Lib to start college, her initial visit to the UNC Pembroke Registrar, taking the Scholastic Aptitude Test (SAT), and being accepted. Here she was, having been out of school for 13-plus years and with four children at home, starting college.

Lib started college in the fall of 1965. In 1966, the family started talking about Ron's call to ministry. During a revival that year, the family went to the front of the church and Ron declared his call to ministry. The result of that family decision was that Lib needed to finish college as soon as possible. Prior to Ron's call to ministry, the plan was that Lib had five years to finish college since that is when Ron Jr. would enter college. That all changed because Lib's income would be needed when Ron left his job to enter full-time ministry.

Lib went to summer school in 1966 carrying 18 hours. From that point on, she was in summer school every summer until graduation. She accumulated hours so quickly that she was never a junior; going from sophomore to senior. In her last semester, Lib completed seven courses, earning six A's and one B. She graduated third in her class. Instead of taking the leisurely five years to graduate, she graduated in 2 years and 9 months. Lib later earned a master's degree in Reading Education.

Prior to their marriage, Ron had completed one year of study at North Carolina State University. He and Lib had agreed that when she finished college, Ron would go back and finish his degree. They executed that plan. Ron's last day with the North Carolina Department of Transportation was 12 September 1968 and he started college on 13 September. He earned his undergraduate degree in Sociology at UNC Pembroke in 1970.

Ron became the pastor of Lake Lynn Baptist Church in September of 1969. Since he had just become a pastor, Ron decided he should not go to seminary immediately. About halfway through the semester, he realized that was a mistake. He completed the paperwork to enter Southeastern Seminary in January 1971. With another pastor, he commuted from Hope Mills to the seminary in

Wake Forest, North Carolina. Ron graduated in December 1974; earning a Master of Divinity (MDiv).

Ron later attended some night classes that were offered at Fort Bragg through Southeastern Seminary. One night, the Registrar announced that students who had been in classes for a couple of years could go into a Doctor of Ministry program. They had enough class work so that they could earn the doctorate by completing the seminars. Ron was working with the South River Baptist Association and was allowed to do the required seminars; earning the doctorate.

The record is clear. Ron and Lib made education a family priority and their doing so benefitted their children and grandchildren, but also their marriage. A comment made by Ron should be considered against the backdrop of all that is presented in this chapter:

"A four-year college degree is important to have and other degrees are, too. However, it is not the number of degrees a person has; it's how we use the education."

Here are some takeaways from this chapter:

1. Having children presents challenges in a marriage that should be acknowledged and addressed.
2. Education, whether college or trade school, is essential to independent living as an adult.
3. There are some issues on which parents should not compromise with children.
4. Parents must start extremely early planning for the education of their children.
5. Successful parenting does not "just happen"; it takes commitment, planning, and hard work.
6. Parents must prepare children to accept responsibility for wrong choices and to take action to successfully move beyond the consequences of those wrong choices.

7. Modeling what is good and right is far more effective than words alone.
8. Education simply for the sake of education is a waste.
9. Above all, build and nurture relationship with God.

CHAPTER EIGHT

NAVIGATING CONFLICT

"Since every marriage has its tensions, it isn't a question of avoiding them but of *how you deal with them*. Conflict can lead to a process that develops oneness or isolation. You and your spouse must choose how you will act when conflict occurs."[1]

Some would expect this chapter to be titled "Resolving Conflict". For me, to resolve a conflict means that the matter is concluded; it is no more. When a court case has gone through all of the appeals and a final decision is rendered, it is over. Hopefully, the litigants go their separate ways and there is no further engagement that requires action or attention. My experience in marriage, and observation of others, make it clear that occurrences of conflict are a constant in marriages. Consequently, there never comes a point at which there is total absence of conflict; no end to challenges to marital peace and closeness. Assuming this view to be accurate, dealing with conflict in marriage is more about finding a way through each occurrence than never having conflict happen. That is the point of the quote at the top of this page.

A salient point from that quote is that the approach chosen by a couple for dealing with conflict can result in "oneness or isolation".

A danger here is that many couples do not intentionally choose a process or approach for dealing with conflict. Instead, they just do what has been ingrained by experiences and exposure to others in marital relationships. Until I met and spent hours talking with Ron and Lib, my only close-up point of reference for addressing conflict in marriage was what I saw with my mother and father. They certainly had not agreed on a positive plan for addressing conflict. Like far too many couples, they did the best they could with what they knew.

Another critical component of having a plan is that both parties in a marriage must commit to and act on the plan. This cannot be a "lip-service" approach on the part of one or both husband and wife. The words must be accompanied by a willingness to work at the agreed upon process and to do so even when the going is tough. I think we live in a time when far too few people are willing to work hard at anything, much less at navigating conflicts in marriage.

A big part of my shortcomings in preparing to navigate conflict in my marriages resulted from not giving anywhere near adequate attention to resources that might have helped. For instance, I recently read "Six Steps for Resolving Conflict in Marriage" on the Family Life website. The six steps were listed and explained. Except for their use of the word "resolving", I found the information extremely helpful as I examine my past marriages and the present one. The six steps are listed below, but a visit to the website and reading of the discussion of each step is strongly recommended and encouraged:

Step One: Resolving conflict requires knowing, accepting, and adjusting to your differences.
Step Two: Resolving conflict requires defeating selfishness.
Step Three: Resolving conflict requires pursuing the other person.
Step Four: Resolving conflict requires loving confrontation.

Step Five: Resolving conflict requires forgiveness.
Step Six: Resolving conflict requires returning a blessing for an insult.[2]

Reflecting on chapters 2-7 of this book portrays numerous instances where Ron and Lib, as needed, employed the steps listed above. Among these would be:

1. **Ron resisting celebration of his birthday, but Lib forthrightly raising the issue with him.**
2. **Ron's father seeing him as "henpecked", but Ron and Lib working through that uneasy situation.**
3. **Lib's extroversion as opposed to Ron's introversion.**

However, Ron relates one instance where every step appears to have come into play. He starts the account by explaining that Lib had a tendency of clamming up, of not arguing. In a situation that might result in an argument, she would stop talking and not say a word. Early on in their marriage, Ron was not sure he was willing to break-in on those periods of silence. He chose to be quiet and let it go.

Then came the time when just the two of them were on a long drive to an engagement where Ron was to speak. He would be addressing a youth group. After being on the road for at least three hours, Lib had not said a word and Ron had followed his normal course of not speaking up. Ron does not remember the reason, but they were angry about something.

Finally, Ron said, "Libby, we have got to work out something here. I can't lead this conference for these youth when I know that you and I are not on speaking terms." That opening statement got them talking about the issue and they settled the matter before they got to their destination.

Ron says that Lib's practice of clamming up and not saying anything probably kept them from making some comments that they would have regretted later. Those comments would have been made out of anger. Lib adds, "I was always afraid I would say too much; so it was better for me to say nothing than say anything."

Ron closes this bit of reflection by saying, "We have learned over time to apologize for whatever we have done unknowingly or intentionally and then begin to talk about it." He and Lib agree that Ron is normally the one who has to break the silence. Ron says that he breaks the silence by saying, "Honey, we really need to talk about this. I can't handle this quiet anymore." With that opening, they talk their way through the situation to, in love, moving on.

I hold that, in that place of disagreement and silence, Lib and Ron addressed every one of the "Six Steps for Resolving Conflict in Marriage". Here is how those steps show up:

1. Long ago, Ron and Lib clearly recognized their differences and both adjusted to them.
2. In the trip experience, although Ron expressed that he could not speak to the youth with this tension between him and Lib unaddressed, his obvious concern was for their relationship and not his presentation. The comment about the presentation was to be clear regarding the importance of addressing the divide between him and his wife.
3. When the time was right, as opposed to previous practice, Ron reached out to Lib.
4. Ron's request to address the situation was presented in loving terms. Lib immediately responded in like fashion. Be reminded, it takes two committed individuals to make this process work.
5. Even though the account does not mention statements of forgiveness, Ron's closing statement in discussing this event says they always address forgiveness.

6. Knowing Ron and Lib, I find it difficult to believe that either of them would knowingly insult the other. Lib's three hours of silence might be seen as an insult. However, her reason for not speaking was because she knew something might be said that would escalate the situation. Be reminded, Ron was also quiet for three hours and later recognized that it was probably good that both of them were quiet for that time. In the end, they satisfied this step by avoiding the need for either of them to honor it.

A bit of an aside is that where married couples do not navigate conflict well, they are not the only ones adversely affected. Everybody, especially children, in the household is negatively impacted. That negative impact can extend even beyond the household. On the other hand, when conflict is handled well, all of those same people benefit. Ron and Lib's daughter, Lisa, once said to them she did not know how to argue in her marriage because she never saw or heard them argue. Ron Jr. added that he assumed Ron and Lib argued, but he never saw or heard it.

I invite readers to think back to those chapters that address Ron and Lib's children as youngsters and as adults. You won't find any indication of the troubling consequences that are routinely visited upon children who grow up watching their parents fail to navigate conflict well.

Let me be crystal clear, conflict will happen in every marriage and the time will never come in any marriage when there is not a single instance of conflict. The discussion in this chapter aims to provide some insights as to how couples might prepare to navigate conflict. Beyond that, the account of how Ron and Lib learned to and executed navigating conflict shows that it can be done. Hopefully, their story provides some instruction and encouragement to couples that are facing challenges in this area.

CHAPTER NINE

CORE VALUES OVER SHARED INTERESTS

"Experts suggest that couples don't have to share many of the same interests to have a long and lasting relationship. If you share many of the same core values, your relationship has a stronger foundation than if it's based purely on a similar taste in music, or other interests that might shift throughout life."[1]

The importance of the statement quoted above should be given serious consideration by persons considering entering a relationship. Further, couples that are already married but have never given meaningful attention to shared values as more important to success in marriage than common interests should visit, or revisit, the matter.

A very good listing of values to be considered, even though it might not be all-inclusive, appears below. The list is from an internet site that can be reached by searching for "Values in a relationship". Each value has a dropdown that defines the value. The link appears in the footnotes at the end of this chapter but it is extremely long. Here is the listing of values:[2]

Communication	**Finance**	**Equality**
Respect	**Loyalty**	**Friendship**
Honesty	**Conflict resolution**	**Empathy**
Trust	**Humor**	**Reliability**
Forgivenes	**Religion**	**Authenticity**
Appreciation	**Work ethic**	**Commitment**
Family	**Emotional support**	**Faith In each Other**
Accountability	**Core beliefs**	**Growth**

There are differences between Ron and Lib regarding interests. One is Ron's enjoyment of being on his computer. He is well-informed, but does not share Lib's love of reading. Yes, they make a point of going to bed at the same time, but, if Ron has trouble sleeping, he will get up and work at his computer. Lib will sit reading a book for hours and spends very little time on a computer.

Further, Ron is one who, at 92 years of age as I am writing this in July 2024, is not intimidated by technical issues. When experiencing some computer problems recently, he did not hesitate to try figuring out what needed to be done. When that failed, he was on the phone seeking assistance and doing so with an attitude of "making corrective action happen". On the other hand, Lib has no substantial interest in computers.

Lib enjoys shopping, especially at Hamrick's. As much as he loves Lib, Ron expresses great appreciation that Carol, who does some house cleaning for them, is happy to drive Lib to Hamrick's and shop with her. Shopping is not of interest to Ron.

Ron and Lib share some interests, but there are some that are held by one, but not the other. The opening quote is correct: shared interests are not a key to this very successful marriage. Rather, a major reason for their success is shared core values. As impossible as it might seem, Ron and Lib have given attention to every entry on that "Values in a relationship" list. I do not know that they identified every one of them and committed to address them; however, a reading of this book makes clear that they believe in, and act on, these key values.

The rest of the story is that Ron and Lib's commitment to adhering to these values helped create a marriage where they could each pursue endeavors outside the home while maintaining closeness and mutual support. Without a doubt, Ron was extremely effective in ministry and thoroughly enjoyed it. Likewise, Lib excelled and found joy in her endeavors outside the home. In addition to what is shared elsewhere in this book regarding Ron's ministry, addressing Lib's experiences shows what is possible when a married couple focuses on core values instead of similar interests.

Lib's working and volunteering outside the home started with her graduation from college. The road to income-producing work came quickly. She did her student teaching at Legion Road Elementary School in Hope Mills, North Carolina. Ed V. Baldwin was the principal. When Lib's student teaching was completed, Ed Baldwin came to her and said, "Miss Loftis, I don't know if you have found a job or not, but I am going to have an opening. If you would like to work here, I can put you on next year." He promised to call Lib as soon as he received the current teacher's resignation. He did what he promised. That was her first teaching job.

Ed Baldwin proved to be a very capable and effective principal. In fact, the school's name was later changed from Legion Road Elementary to Ed V. Baldwin Elementary in his honor.

This was the start of Lib's 30 year teaching career. She admits to loving teaching. That love of teaching is not limited to educational institutions. She brings that same vigor and commitment to any teaching endeavor. At 91 years of age, her love of teaching shows through as she still teaches a Sunday school class.

Lib describes her approach to teaching as giving students materials and having them follow as she explains them. She says this is not what happens, for instance, when she asks someone to teach her an action to be performed on her mobile phone. They take the phone and start talking "a mile a minute". Her preference is to keep her phone and practice on it what the other person is doing on their phone. Clearly, Lib is a seasoned teacher.

This love of teaching and the pure joy that she has known and continues to experience comes alive as she shares teaching experiences. For example, pure excitement comes through as she talks about spending time in the part of Brazil that is in the Southern Hemisphere. When back home teaching a group of students, she was able to, based on first-hand experience, explain that water draining from a sink in the Southern Hemisphere circles in the opposite direction of water draining in the Northern Hemisphere.

A major turning point in Lib's teaching career came during her employment at Southview Middle School in Hope Mills, North Carolina. It was there that the principal offered her an opportunity to become a reading instructor. Her work in that area led to training in the Laubach method described below:

> ***"The Laubach method was developed specifically to help adults with limited or no reading skills achieve success and become confident readers. This structured, phonics-based series works even with learners who have had negative experiences with other reading programs."***[3]

After some initial preparation for this assignment, Lib completed extensive Laubach training at Samford University in Homewood, Alabama. This involved 10 days of study on how to work with adults who do not know how to read or write. The training included preparation for working with non-English speaking students. Following that training, she started doing some teaching in the Fayetteville area using the Laubach method.

Using the Laubach method in teaching was obviously a very satisfying experience for Lib. With pure excitement, she shares a couple of accounts from that time.

The first account happened while Ron was working as the Director of Christian Social Ministries with New South River Baptist Association in Cumberland County, North Carolina. The Association arranged to assist a Vietnamese family in settling in the area. The Kim family had been brought to America as part of the relocation effort after the war in Viet Nam. The group included a husband and wife, their nine children, along with the wife's brother and niece. Ron was the sponsor for this family. That meant that he made arrangements for getting them settled in the area; including registering the children in school.

This group had spent two years in a camp before coming to Fayetteville and had learned a bit of English during that time. However, they needed help to become much more fluent in English. Lib was able to assist them in achieving a higher level of fluency. This was in 1979 and 1980. Even though they moved from the Fayetteville area, across all the years since the interaction between Ron, Lib, and the Kim family, members of the family have stayed in touch with Ron and Lib. The niece and her husband were traveling through Fayetteville in 2022 and made it a point to stop and visit with Ron and Lib.

The close connection with the Kim family that shows through above was not limited to Ron and Lib. Their son, Steve, and daughter, Lisa, were very involved in assisting the newly arrived family. Steve was about to begin his junior year at Wake Forest University and Lisa was a rising senior in high school. Lisa assisted with the needs of the small girls and Steve helped with the older boys. Both of them helped their group prepare for adjusting to life in America.

Steve remained in contact with children and grandchildren of the family via social media. In the 2016 timeframe, he received an invitation from the Kim family for some members of the Loftis family to visit them in Florida. In response, Steve, his wife Lee, their sons Matthew and Colin, Lisa and her daughter Holly, Lib and Ron made the trip to Tampa, Florida. It was quite a reunion. Steve, Lisa, and Ron stay in touch with the family through social media.

Here is an aside consideration. The focus in this chapter is on Ron and Lib and their attention to appropriate core values. The actions across the years of their son and daughter, along with those of the Kim family, show the possibility of passing commitment to appropriate core values on from one generation to another. Many of the values listed in the opening of this chapter show up in the conduct of both the Loftis and Kim families. When a husband and wife live based on appropriate core values, their children will very likely take on those values.

The second account is of a man who drove an 18-wheeler cross country making deliveries and pick-ups, but could not read or write. He joined one of Lib's classes. Realizing that he was a truck driver who traveled all over America, Lib asked him how he found his way to various destinations. He explained that he could follow highway numbers by seeing them on a map. Upon arriving in a city, he would stop at a business and ask for directions. This student learned to read and write. He went on to more advanced training.

Again, Lib lights up and her face and voice show pure joy, absolute happiness, as she shares these experiences. Those are just two stories among almost limitless positive experiences that Lib had while using the Laubach method to teach reading and writing across America.

In 1994, Lib concluded her classroom teaching career at W.H. Knuckles Elementary School in Lumberton, North Carolina;

she retired. This school was located in a low-income area with a substantial number of children from single-parent households headed by an unmarried mother. Lib enjoyed the students and that teaching experience. After all of the years since her retirement, some of the students she taught at Knuckles Elementary are still in touch. One who is married and has children has visited Lib in the past couple of years.

Without doubt, Lib had a very successful and personally enjoyable career as a classroom teacher and in teaching reading using the Laubach method. Even during her teaching career, Lib was involved with Ron in his ministry. In addition to her work with the Kim family that Ron sponsored, Lib assisted Ron with presenting mission studies that addressed the Christian witness and its impact in the world. These presentations were made to churches that were affiliated with the Association. Ron would often receive calls from individuals who wanted to schedule a class and thought that he would be teaching it. Instead, he responded that Lib would be the teacher.

Lib estimates that she conducted 35-40 of these classes. She shares that a friend, Sudie, would often go with her when she was teaching a class. Someone asked Sudie if she ever got tired of hearing the same things over-and-over. She responded that Lib never did classes the same way; consequently, there was no repetition.

Lib also served as director of the Woman's Missionary Union (WMU) for the Association. The WMU mission is, "Challenging, preparing and equipping Christian believers to be radically involved in the fulfillment of the Great Commission".[4] She held this position for many years and could have continued; but at age 80, concluded it was time to retire. She says, "I had been there long enough and some new blood needed to get in."

Lib's retirement from classroom teaching in 1994 came as Ron was starting his second time as the pastor of Lake Lynn Baptist

Church. At Lake Lynn, Lib became even more involved in doing ministry with Ron. She was Minister of Music and, over time, taught adults in a couple of Sunday school classes. Ron says that their doing some ministry work together made it easier for them to adjust to being together in their senior years.

The verbal picture painted here is of a lady who, to this day, has had, and continues to have, a life filled with excitement about and pure enjoyment of living. Ron's past and present reflect the same level of excitement and pure enjoyment of living as does Lib's. When I look at all of what is presented here, the revelation for me is that, without peace and harmony in their marital relationship, the amazingly wonderful life experiences that they had, and are having, outside the home would not have been, and would not be, possible.

Reflecting on all that is presented above, my realization now is that what happens in a marriage impacts, for good or bad, every aspect of a person's life. That impact is not limited to interactions between a husband and wife. For instance, being unhappy and frustrated in one's workplace might have less to do with the job situation than with a stressful and troubled marriage. The condition of a marriage might even affect one's health. The following speaks to the climate of a marriage affecting life beyond the marriage itself:

> **"Our personal relationships are our greatest source of pleasure. Which also means they are our greatest source of pain. So when things go wrong in our marriages or intimate relationships, the resulting stress can be extremely significant. For some, even debilitating.**
>
> **This stress can impact all other areas of our lives – including work. Increased stress levels lead to poor decision-making, ineffective communication, impaired memory and bad time management. The**

> **constant thoughts of all the relationship issues can make it difficult to focus and reduce productivity. The overall result is poor work performance – which could have a disastrous effect on your career. Knowing your work performance is below par, and your career could be on the line, naturally induces even more stress. Stress which you then take home with you. And possibly unleash on your partner. And then the cycle continues…"[5]**

Ron and Lib Loftis provide proof-positive that building a proper foundation of a values-based marriage is essential to positively impacting the lives of marital partners in the home, but also in every aspect of life. Not only does their experience show that it works; there is much "how to" in their story. My hope is that, in marriage, readers will follow the lead of Ron and Lib; focused on core values, not on shared interests.

CHAPTER TEN

Positively Touching the Lives of Others

"Love is not words, it's actions, and love isn't feelings, it's a decision."
Steven Furtick

Love of others drives us to positively touch the lives of people both near and far from us. This is the command and example of Jesus. He says:

> **"You shall love the Lord your God with all your heart, with all your soul, and with all your mind. This is the first and great commandment. And the second is like it: You shall love your neighbor as yourself." (Matthew 22:37-39, New King James Version)**

From chapter 9, this is about one's relationship with God; about religion. In my estimation, this is the core value that impacts the extent to which a person engages the other values listed in the opening of that chapter. The words of Steven Furtick quoted above are absolutely true. It is not love to simply speak the good sounding words, but not accompany them with loving actions. Good feelings do not produce meaningful actions; it does require deciding to act.

Lib and Ron provide crystal clear guidance regarding how love in action looks; how one might come to love as Jesus commanded. Giving attention to how each of them came to the point of loving others and acting on that love can be instructive. As with other points raised in this book, one might wonder what loving others has to do with building a successful marriage. In answering that question, consider the following from Ashlynn Larsen:

> **"In the maze of human experience, love finds its way through every aspect of our lives, enriching our existence in myriad ways. Research within positive psychology has highlighted the correlation between love and happiness, with individuals in loving relationships reporting higher life satisfaction (Hendrick & Hendrick, 2017). The benefits of love extend to physical health, with lower blood pressure and reduced cardiovascular disease risk observed in individuals in loving relationships (Gerard, 2019). Furthermore, supportive relationships rich in love can be associated with resilience and longevity. However, despite all the benefits love has on our lives, amidst the hustle and bustle of daily life, we often overlook the profound depth and abundance of love that surrounds us. From the warmth of platonic relationships to the kindness of strangers, love manifests itself in diverse forms, shaping our well-being and contributing to our overall life satisfaction."[1]**

I hold that the statement above is totally accurate. Our "well-being and overall life satisfaction" are clearly affected by the extent to which we love others. Granted, getting the full benefit of loving others requires a two-way relationship. However, loving others and acting on it has a way of creating a loving atmosphere that others are drawn into.[2] I contend that Ron and Lib's experience confirms this assessment as being true. What follows are some considerations that indicate the positive impact on Ron and Lib from loving others.

A discussion starting point is how they came to love others. Lib explains her journey by sharing an experience that she had with her mother. She got lice at school and brought them home, infecting her sisters. Her mother was unhappy about that outcome because she had the chore of getting rid of the lice. She said to Lib, "You have got to quit loving on people. You just love everybody you see." Interestingly, Lib says that maybe her loving other people might have been passed from her mother. Despite her response to Lib bringing lice home, Lib's mother loved other people and acted on that love. Be reminded at this point of what is said in chapter 9 about core values being passed on to children. Then, no matter how Lib was introduced to loving others, she still had to choose to act on it.

On the other hand, Ron says that, as a child, love of others was not part of his make-up. He loved his parents and others who were close to him. Loving others beyond that small group was not on his radar. It was an experience in the first church that he pastored that awakened him to the need for giving attention to loving others. He was still working for the North Carolina Department of Transportation while pastoring that church. That made for a demanding and physically draining routine. It was a long drive from their home to the church. They made that trip twice on Sundays for worship and again on Wednesday nights for Bible study.

There were three churches in the community where Ron was pastoring: Presbyterian, AME Zion, and Ron's Baptist church. Ron's church was the only one that held vacation Bible school during the summer. This was 1969, while the Civil Rights Movement was active and America was racially divided and very tense because of that condition. In the midst of this situation, Ron recommended that his church invite children from the other two churches to participate in the vacation Bible school. Ron says, "That was not exactly the thing to do in 1969." The problem was that his church was an all-white congregation, as was the Presbyterian Church, while the AME Zion Church was all-black.

The Chairman of the Deacons could not read or write, but he found ways to hide it. Because of Ron's Bible school suggestion, this chairman held a secret deacons' meeting to organize opposition to Ron continuing as pastor. Before his time as pastor, the church had gone through a difficult split and Ron did not want to be part of that happening again. Consequently, he resigned effective 1 July 1969.

Ron came away from that experience with some very angry feelings toward that chairman. In calm reflection, Ron recognized that the chairman was operating out of his illiteracy and his racial bias from years past. Ron says he had to learn to forgive the chairman for what he did by way of trying to have him terminated as pastor. Ron does not know if he came to love that man, but the experience did lead him to understand why the chairman attempted the termination. It was because of his illiteracy and racial bias. That experience led Ron to being able to love people who disagree with him.

Ron goes on to say that he was making a change from a secular vocation to a spiritual vocation. He thought, "Ronald, you can't be a pastor if you are going to hold these kinds of grudges against people." Again, here is the decision to love others and to act on that decision.

Let's move on now to some instances where Ron and Lib's love for others showed through. While Ron was serving as Director of Missions with the Robeson Baptist Association, he made his first trip to Brazil. This was an orientation trip for directors of missions from several Baptist associations. Robinson Baptist Association had committed to missionary outreach to people in Brazil. Each member of the group was assigned an interpreter.

Ron and the others from America were in a group where the speaker presented in Portuguese and English. Newton Vidal was sitting near Ron. He was an attorney who appeared to only understand Portuguese. He was also a Baptist minister. After the group meeting, the attendees walked to lunch together. As they were walking, Newton walked up next to Ron and started talking in English. Ron said, "Newton, you speak English as well as you speak Portuguese." Newton responded, "No, not quite as well, Ronald." He and Ron became close friends. He was the contact person every time the Association sent a team to Brazil.

Newton came to America several times and stayed at the Loftis' home. One visit lasted six weeks. On Sundays, Ron would take Newton to various churches and he would be the speaker. Newton taught Ron a few key words in Portuguese. During sermons, Newton would pretend he did not know those words in English and would have Ron interpret. It was a fun exercise. Newton began learning English at a Billy Graham Crusade in Europe. That was followed by listening to recordings.

Lib talks about Newton planning their day. He would go to work with Ron and Lib was off to her teaching job. Before that, they would talk about what they were going to do that day. At times, there would be something the three of them were going to do together. When Lib would interject an item for the day's plan, Newton would often say, "Ron, you are the boss, but Lib is the queen." In other words, Lib's input outranked Ron's. Knowing about the town of Newton Grove near Fayetteville and Elizabethtown, another city near Fayetteville, Newton said, "Ron, why don't they have a Ronaldtown. In unison, Ron and Lib say, "It was a perfect relationship."

Working together with Newton Vidal and the Brazilian effort continued until Ron left his Association position in 1994 to become pastor again at Lake Lynn Baptist Church. Ron and Lib's son, Steve, made a trip to Brazil and Newton was his sponsor.

On Newton Vidal's last visit to the Loftis' home, he was very sick with a really bad cold. Ron took him to the doctor twice. He ended up returning home to Brazil, but died shortly after getting there.

I never met Newton Vidal; only saw one photo of him. However, writing about the relationship between him, Lib, and Ron and knowing that I had to come to that last paragraph caused me to start crying halfway through the account. On the one hand, I am sad for the ending; but on the other, I celebrate the tremendous love these three people obviously had for one another and how their lives were blessed beyond description by that love.

When we love others and choose to act on it, I think over time, loving responses become almost automatic. Lib and Ron were visiting their daughter, Lisa, who lives in the mountains of North Carolina. Lisa took them to an apple farm. They picked apples and told the owner that the plan was to give each member of their Sunday school classes an apple. The owner, a lady, would not accept payment for the apples.

Lib decided to bake a pound cake for the orchard owner. Lisa had all the needed ingredients. She made the cake and left it with Lisa for delivery. After Ron and Lib returned home, Lisa delivered the cake. The orchard owner called Lisa and said, "Do you think there is any possibility I could get this recipe?" The owner explained that she wanted to make pound cakes and sell them. She had been trying recipes without finding one that was right to sell. However, when she bit into Lib's cake, she knew that was the one. Lisa said she was sure Lib would share the recipe.

The lady said she would have to put Lib's name on the cake. She and Lisa discussed what to put on it. Lisa said, "Grandma Lib's Pound Cake." That's what it is. Interestingly, Lib got the recipe out of a newspaper. Making and giving that pound cake was an automatic response because of Lib's love for others.

When Ron retired from pastoring, he and Lib were ready to find a church where they could be members, but slow their pace. Ed Beddingfield was pastor at First Baptist Church on Anderson Street in Fayetteville. Ron and Lib had known Beddingfield since he first came to the area in 1980 as pastor of Mount Pisgah Baptist Church. Ron had lunch with Beddingfield and talked about him and Lib joining First Baptist. The pastor assured Ron that having another preacher in the Church would not be a problem. Beddingfield was very welcoming. Ron and Lib joined First Baptist.

Their thought was that the two of them, after so many years of ministry, would join a Sunday school class and sit together and enjoy the experience of having someone else teach. For Lib, that lasted exactly three Sundays. On the third Sunday, a lady who was teaching one of the classes for elderly ladies came to Lib and asked if she would teach the class for her. The lady said she and her husband had bought an Airstream trailer and her husband wanted to travel that summer. Lib explained that she had not been at the Church long enough to think about teaching a class. She promised to think about and pray regarding the request.

Lib talked with the pastor, Ed Beddingfield, and his advice was that she agree to teach just for the summer. Lib decided that she would commit to teach for the summer. On a Sunday shortly after the conversation with Ed Beddingfield, Lib was waiting to see the lady so that she could give her commitment to teach for the summer. Coming toward Lib with the next quarter's Sunday school books in her hands, the teacher says to Lib, "I am not coming back to this class", and gave the books to Lib.

Lib responded by asking herself and asking God, "What do you do...leave that class without a teacher?" That is the kind of question asked by a person who loves others and is prepared to take action in support of them as deemed appropriate. Lib went on to teach that class until participation substantially declined due to deaths of members. She says, "Participants left the class and were promoted directly to Heaven." Lib went on to teach other Sunday school classes and is teaching a class to this day, 12 July 2024.

Beyond teaching Sunday school, Lib has served as a deacon. In fact, she was Chair of Deacons when the current pastor, Rob James, was called. She has been, and continues to be, a leader in the Woman's Missionary Union (WMU) at First Baptist.

Like Lib, Ron came to First Baptist expecting a much slower pace than turned out to be the case. He has served several tours on the Deacon Board and was on the Search Committee when Rob James was called as pastor. He has helped plan various Christian education efforts in the Church and taught some courses.

Ron's primary effort now is serving as teacher of the Ladies' Sunday School Class. It was approximately 2011 when this class was established and Ron became the teacher. David Best was assistant pastor at First Baptist. His wife, Jane, suggested to David that a class was needed for ladies who were not married and those whose husbands did not come to church or husbands were busy with church assignments and not available for Sunday school. David approached Ron about teaching such a class and he agreed to do so. The class started with four women in it.

Attendance in that class grew, although slowly. After several years, a group of ladies from another church joined First Baptist and most of them started attending the Ladies' Class. When this group started attending, Ron says, "Members of the class just kind of swarmed around them." I have observed this class in session. They are joy-filled and show great love and appreciation for one another. Ron says that he gives them 15 minutes to fellowship at the start of class and then starts the discussion. He goes on to say that the class has been, and still is, a great blessing to him.

Speaking for himself, with Lib's obvious concurrence, Ron says:

> **"Instead of spending our retirement sitting on a chair or in a pew twiddling our thumbs, we have been pretty busy. We have a deep sense of gratitude to God for giving us that opportunity and the physical ability to do all that we have, and are doing, at First Baptist."**

All that has been shared above regarding Ron and Lib's involvement at First Baptist is further testimony to their love of people. However, there is a final consideration in this matter of loving others. There are times when love requires us to walk away from actions that we view as loving, even know them to be loving. Ron and Lib realize that the physical challenges that they are facing in their very senior years dictate that they give up teaching their Sunday school classes. They could continue teaching while doing so at a level they know to be less than what is effective and deserved by their students. Some would continue because of selfish reasons such as being recognized, feeling some level of importance, and so forth. This is not the case with Ron and Lib Loftis; no, they act out of love for others and under God's direction. Consequently, they are moving to turn their classes over to others who are able to carry on in an appropriate manner.

So, because others are positively responsive, this love of others does for Ron and Lib exactly what appears at the end of the Ashlynn Larsen quote referenced earlier in this chapter: "**From the warmth of platonic relationships to the kindness of strangers,**

love manifests itself in diverse forms, shaping our well-being and contributing to our overall life satisfaction."[3] Our well-being and overall life satisfaction impact how we respond in a marital relationship. Consequently, the extent to which a person loves others and allows that love to produce God-consistent actions affects the success of one's marriage. Again, Ron and Lib are bright shining models of how this process looks when it happens.

CHAPTER ELEVEN

VIVIAN...THE ULTIMATE IN SHARED MINISTRY

"When couples choose to unselfishly serve others together, they experience peace, contentment and a deeper bond that strengthens their marriage."[1]

Ron and Lib Loftis have spent over 60 years working together in serving others. Without a doubt, as stated in the quote above, their marriage has been, and continues to be, positively impacted by that joint service to others. Whether Lib and Ron were working together in a church where Ron was pastor, or in endeavors under the auspices of an association of churches, their marriage benefitted from that service. That joint service to others continues now as both of them are over 90 years of age. However, there is one joint ministry that deserves substantial attention in this chronicling of their amazing marriage and what others might learn from it. That is their relationship with, and pouring into the life of, a lady named Vivian.

In March 1978, Ron's father became critically ill. Margaret, his stepmother, was a semi-invalid being cared for by his father. His father went into the hospital. Ron and his sister, Marilyn, alternated spending time with him at the hospital.

Given that their father was hospitalized, someone needed to stay with Margaret. Her oldest sister, Joanne, came and stayed with her. However, Joanne required being off on weekends. Looking for someone who could stay with Margaret on the weekend, Ron went to see Alberta Green who had a facility for women suffering with alcoholism. He asked if she had someone who might help with Margaret.

Ron had met Alberta through his work at New South River Baptist Association as Director of Christian Social Ministries. She was director of the association's Samaritan Good Will Center, a men and women's home for alcoholics. Ron explained to Alberta his situation and asked if she could help. She responded that there was a lady who had just checked in that might be a candidate for assisting Ron's stepmother. That lady was Vivian.

After talking further with Alberta and meeting Vivian, Ron took her out to meet Margaret. It was quickly obvious that the two of them could work together. Vivian started caring for Margaret and all went very well. Vivian had just the right temperament for getting Margaret to do what was needed, such as taking her medications. So Joann was with Margaret during the week and Ron would pick Vivian up on Friday from Alberta's facility and drive her back on Sunday afternoon.

After a while, Joann requested that she and Vivian switch days. They did. Vivian was there weekdays and Joanne on the weekend. With Vivian only being at Alberta's facility on the weekends, Alberta explained to Ron that she could not hold a bed for Vivian with her only being there two nights a week. In the face of this difficulty, Ron and Lib moved Vivian into their basement that had a bedroom and bathroom.

That became a time of bonding between Vivian and the Loftis family. The closeness that developed shows through in so many ways, some of them rather simple in appearance. For instance, Lib and Ron would go out for dinner on Friday nights. They started inviting Vivian to go along. She did not know a lot about social graces. Ron would suggest that Lib and Vivian get dressed for dinner. Lib would change from her "school teacher clothes" and put on something more fitting for dinner.

Vivian was accustomed to very casual dress. At Margaret's home, which was rather private, she could wear shorts and t-shirts with all kinds of designs on the shirts. However, that attire was not very appropriate for going out to dinner. Given what Ron and Lib came to know of Vivian's life journey, they chose to offer her help rather than declare her lost and walk away.

As best as Ron and Lib have been able to determine, Vivian was the youngest in a large family of girls. When she was 14, a 21 year-old man took her as his wife. He moved her to his parents' home and she became an unpaid laborer for his parents. Her husband joined the military and she very seldom saw him. She lived with that family and worked on the farm. She gave birth to a daughter and two sons, but to Ron and Lib's knowledge, was not in contact with them during the early several years that they knew her.

Vivian

That bit of background speaks to how Vivian was when Ron and Lib were dealing with her early in the relationship. Knowing Vivian's background, Ron and Lib decided that they would have to walk gently alongside her and teach her what was necessary while having genuine love and concern show through. On the other hand, Vivian would have to recognize the genuineness of Ron and Lib's love and concern; then respond by taking actions to improve her life circumstances. So, in what might appear a minor occurrence, Vivian learned to dress appropriately for those Friday night dinner outings; even looked forward to and thoroughly enjoyed every one of them.

Vivian also came to understand her need for relationship with God through Jesus Christ. She was familiar with the church where Alberta Green took her residents. Although she could have gone to First Baptist with Lib, she chose to keep attending that church. Because Ron was often preaching at various churches, he did not go to First Baptist with Lib on a regular basis. Consequently, Lib would take Vivian to Alberta's church and go on to First Baptist. After worship, she would pick Vivian up from Alberta's facility. Lib says Vivian would be sitting in a swing on the porch.

Ron and Lib were not simply helping an employee; they were unselfishly serving a person in need; in great need.

Over time, Joanne faded from being available to care for Margaret on weekends. Vivian moved into a spare bedroom at Margaret's home and became her full-time caregiver. She did a superb job of caring for Margaret.

At 5:30 one morning, Vivian called Ron and said, "Rev., she's gone." Ron got up and went over. He called Marilyn, his sister, and she came to the house. At one point, Ron reached for the sheet to pull it up over his stepmother's face. In a tone reflecting love and respect for Margaret, Vivian said, "Don't do that; don't cover her up." Ron stopped and did not cover Margaret's face.

In light of Ron's stepmother's death, one might expect that Vivian would go back to Alberta's facility and have no further close contact with Ron and Lib. I repeat: **"Ron and Lib were not simply helping an employee; they were unselfishly serving a person in need; in great need."** After Margaret's death, Vivian moved back to Ron and Lib's home. She spent some time caring for Marilyn's mother-in-law until she died.

Vivian loved the Loftis children. When the children went away to college, but were coming home on a weekend, Vivian would say, "Tell them to bring their laundry." If they were bringing guests, she would say, "Tell the guests to bring their laundry, too." On Saturday during one of those visits, she did laundry all day, folding and placing it in a bag.

A humorous but defining point came when Lib finished a couple of weeks of the Laubach Reading Program training at Samford University in Alabama. So that she would not have to take a bus home, Ron, Lisa, and Vivian drove to Alabama to pick Lib up. They stayed overnight before heading home. Lisa and Vivian shared a room while Ron and Lib were in another room. That night, Lisa, who was 16, and Vivian played with Play-Doh to the point of getting some stuck on the ceiling. They had fun.

Vivian loved Ron, Lib, and their children; and they loved her.

Then came Ron's acceptance of a job with the Home Mission Board Southern Baptist Convention with headquarters in Atlanta, Georgia. Ron and Lib moved to the Atlanta area. Vivian went to live with Marilyn and her husband. When that arrangement did not work out, Ron and Lib moved Vivian to their home in Georgia. She had gotten a driver's license. Lib had a car that was not so great, but worked well for just getting around the local area. They purchased a new car and gave Lib's car to Vivian.

Vivian got a job cleaning houses for individuals. One of her clients was the owner of a funeral home. She worked for other homeowners and did well. At one point, Vivian shared that since everybody she served as a caregiver for died, she needed a different line of work. Vivian cleaned houses the whole time that she, Ron, and Lib were in Georgia.

After 18 months in Georgia, Ron, Lib, and Vivian returned to North Carolina. They were living near Fairmont, which is south of Fayetteville. Ron had accepted the position of Director of Missions with the Robeson Baptist Association headquartered in Lumberton, North Carolina. He and Lib were attending Centerville Baptist Church. They realized that Vivian wanted to get out on her own. The Centerville pastor's mother had a vacant mobile home on her property and was willing to rent it. At a very reasonable monthly rent, Vivian moved into that home. She lived alone while working various jobs.

Vivian was working for a young lady that Ron and Lib knew who lived in the Fairmont area. She hired Vivian to clean her home. The lady called Ron one day and said that she had not seen or heard from Vivian in several days. They agreed to meet at Vivian's mobile home. Upon arriving, they found all of the doors locked. They managed to get in and there was Vivian on the floor. They called EMS and she was taken to the hospital. She stayed in the hospital's alcohol section for 30 days. A young man who worked in that section told Ron that if he and her employer had not found Vivian when they did, she would have died. Further, if she were to start drinking again, she would die of alcoholism.

When Ron checked Vivian out of the hospital, he told her what that young man had said. One weekend some time later, he went by to see how Vivian was doing. He found that she had been drinking. Acknowledging that he was not very nice and that he was angry at her, Ron recalls saying: "Vivian, we were told that if you got onto another drunken spell, you would die of alcoholism. Now you are back here drinking beer again. Vivian, here is what I am going to do if you drink again. I am going to put your ass in my car and drive you to Danville, Virginia. I am going to stop in front of your daughter's house. I am going to put you out and say, 'Here, she is yours.'" To Ron's knowledge, Vivian never drank again. Ron says that he was so upset and Vivian was broken-hearted that she had hurt him.

By this time, Vivian had purchased a mobile home. She was able to make that purchase because of continuing to work various part-time jobs, but also because she received her husband's Social Security after his death. Although they had not been in touch or lived together for years, they never got a divorce. She also became a member of Centerville Baptist Church.

After Vivian was in her purchased mobile home, Ron and Lib had a home built in Hope Mills, North Carolina. The covenants in the new neighborhood did not allow fences. Consequently, they were not able to have their Irish setter, Shannon, be outside. Vivian offered to take and care for the dog. She had a fence installed so that Shannon could be outside.

Ron stopped by one day and there Vivian was, sitting on the ground with her legs crossed and Shannon's head on her lap. This dog that she obviously loved was sick. Vivian sat there and patted Shannon until she died. As Ron and Lib finish telling the story, they say in unison, "That was Vivian."

Eventually, one of Vivian's sons came to live with her. Ron and Lib stayed in touch with her. Vivian developed breast cancer and had to undergo radiation treatments. The radiation was burning her chest so badly that she stopped the treatments and just stayed at home. On Christmas Day in 2001, Ron was visiting someone in the hospital. He received a call from Vivian's son who simply said, "Loftis, Momma just died." Ron went to Vivian's home and arrangements were made for her burial.

A service was held for Vivian in Fairmont, North Carolina, where she lived. Shortly after that, Ron and his son, Steve, conducted a graveside service in Danville, Virginia. Vivian was buried next to her husband. After all those years apart, their earthly bodies were now there side-by-side.

Along with Ron and Steve, Ronald Jr. and Michael (Mike) attended the graveside service in Danville. After all the years since

Vivian's death, Lib explains, with a tone and facial expression showing tremendous sorrow, that their daughter Lisa could not attend either service. That was because her daughter, Holly, was born just 17 days before Vivian died and could not travel. Even further, Lib laments that Vivian never got to see Holly. That lament is deepened by Vivian's love for the Loftis children and her close relationship with them; be reminded of that Play-Doh incident in Alabama with Vivian and Lisa.

I close this chapter as it opened. That is, contending that marriages benefit tremendously from couples "unselfishly serving others together". Listening to Ron and Lib reflect on their times of service to others grabbed my attention and was profoundly instructional. That was especially the case as they talked about Vivian.

For me, the greatest lesson to be learned from Ron and Lib in this area of, as a couple, serving others is to act out of love for people. The second is to act unselfishly. That is, serve without the expectation of, or desire for, any personal gain. Finally, be in agreement on where, when, and how to serve. These three elements do not represent all that should be present as a couple acts to serve others. However, reflection on all of Ron and Lib's efforts in serving others, certainly their actions toward and for Vivian, show that these three elements are essential.

Let the record be clear that, along with other critical factors, because of their service to others, Ron and Lib's marriage has experienced, and continues to experience: peace, contentment, and a deeper bond that strengthens their marriage.

CHAPTER TWELVE

GROWING OLD TOGETHER

“What if you could look at the aging process with joy and expectancy? The concept of conscious aging teaches us to accept ourselves as we age, live with a sense of purpose and let go of what society deems ‘appropriate’ for our stage in life.”[1]

Sitting and talking with Ron and Lib Loftis is, even months later, a blessing beyond description. Time and again, I was amazed, inspired, and instructed by what they shared in our conversations. Part of my being impacted in that fashion was due to them speaking casually, matter-of-factly, about circumstances with which so many people struggle. Among the areas of struggle is that of growing old; of having one’s body go through the changes that come with advanced years. They have, and are, navigating this period together in a manner that greatly benefits their marriage and offers instruction and encouragement to others.

Ronald W. Loftis, Sr. and Elizabeth C. Loftis

As I have also found in my state of growing old, Ron and Lib started realizing that there were things they could no longer do. They got tired quickly; would go into a room and forget why they went in there. They needed help to get up from being seated; Ron relies on the arms of his chair and Lib's main chair lifts her to her feet. As they recognized these changes, Lib would quote part of the opening from Robert Browning's poem, "Rabbi Ben Ezra": "Grow old along with me! The best is yet to be..." After quoting that segment, she would say, "That's a lot of malarkey."

Ron shares that bit regarding Lib's initial response to her recognition of growing old. Then he says that they moved from seeing that statement as being questionable to experiencing it as a reality in their marriage. Even in the midst of physical decline, their relationship kept getting "better and better".

Ron's "better and better" assessment of their relationship in these senior years reflects the truth put forth in the remainder of that quote from Robert Browning's poem. In full, it says: "Grow old along with me! The best is yet to be, the last of life, for which the first was made." Ron and Lib are experiencing exactly what Browning wrote. They conducted the "first" of their marriage in a loving, God-fearing manner and maintain that condition now. By "God-fearing", I mean loving God and seeking, day in and day out, to live as He calls us to live. Because of what they did in the foundational years, their "last of life" is "better and better." The warning here is do not, in a marriage, expect that the first part can be filled with strife and discord, with a lack of loving actions, and expect the last part will be blissful. Without a doubt, a dismal start to a marriage can be overcome with demanding effort, but why not follow Lib and Ron's pattern; start strong and grow even stronger over time.

Even in these very senior years, they have not ceased being active. Ron says, "Instead of spending our retirement sitting on a chair and in a pew twiddling our thumbs, we have been pretty busy." As indicated in various sections of this book, since retirement and to this time, both have continued to teach Sunday school classes and have been in various other leadership and teaching roles. Again, Ron expresses gratitude to God for giving Lib and him the opportunity to keep serving and being active.

Lib shares a critical consideration regarding a proper mindset for growing old. She says:

> **"Growing old has really not been an issue for us. I think we have kind of looked forward to a time when we weren't swamped with responsibilities like teaching school, pastoring a church, or any of the myriad of other responsibilities."**

People said Ron and Lib would be absolutely miserable when Lisa, their youngest child, went to college. They were not at all miserable. Lib says, "For the first time in our lives, we had each other and that was all we had to worry about at home. We could go when we wanted to go and where we wanted to go." Lisa was in college and enjoying the experience. They were definitely not miserable; they were able to embrace their new circumstance. They took on a right mindset for that new phase of life.

As has been the case across the years, they recognize, respect, and accept what is different between them. Ron explains that he likes to read, but finds it hard to sit and read for long periods. After 20-30 minutes, he has to get up and spend time on some other task. Lib, on the other hand, can sit and read for hours. Now that they are together 24 hours a day, 7 days a week, a difference such as this could be a problem. It is not, however, because in this area, as well as with other differences, they have recognized the benefit of "giving space" to each other. On the other hand, where differences deserve being addressed, they are addressed in an atmosphere of love and respect. This point is critical not only in the latter years of a marriage, but throughout.

In retirement, Ron and Lib are able to have a different schedule from when they were working. During those working years, their schedules made it difficult to have the kind of time together that is possible now. They make it a point to include relationship-building actions even after all their years of marriage. They go to bed at the same time and get up about the same time; do not go to sleep without a hug and "I love you". In the morning, there is a tight hug and a kiss. They say that all of this is truer now than in those pre-retirement years. One might think that this kind of closeness would be more prevalent in the early years and fade or disappear in the senior years. Therein is another tidbit for consideration.

Be careful not to read the preceding paragraph as being totally about mere physical contact and a routine statement of love. It is important to understand that these interactions occur in the presence of real love that is not dependent on physical contact; but is simply expressed in that contact and spoken words. Ron explains this as he describes a time of deep thought during his recovery from surgery:

> **"I was sitting in the sunroom watching the birds feed; one thing or another. My whole life had changed. All of that action was gone. I could get up and be around the house. You do a lot of thinking. Your mind runs in all kinds of directions; mine does anyway. All sexual activity had been cut-off some few years earlier. I was 88 years old when I had the surgery done. Somehow, in all of that, I thought about a zillion things. One thing I thought about was my relationship with Lib. I had gotten to the point now where the children felt safe leaving us at home by ourselves. I realized it was**

> **just Lib and me. (Long pause) I think in all of that, it occurred to me that all this romantic stuff has been replaced with a spiritual unity between Lib and me. It must have been a thought of God's love for us and how much that is just a pure true love; without taking anything else into consideration."**

Ron and Lib's love for each other is "pure true love". The physical actions and spoken words reflect and indicate the presence of that "pure true love".

In their senior years, Ron and Lib are doing exactly what that opening quote recommends: "...accept ourselves as we age, live with a sense of purpose and let go of what society deems 'appropriate' for our stage in life."

So, there it is; 12 chapters that, hopefully, paint a word picture of a "Marriage for the Ages". It is a marriage that brings alive that line from Robert Browning's poem, "The best is yet to be, the last of life, for which the first was made." In their marriage, Ron and Lib Loftis demonstrate, for all of us, that the blissful relationship that Browning suggests can be made real. My hope and prayer is that Ron and Lib's story will, for readers, prove amazing, inspiring, and instructional -as it does for me.

EPILOGUE

Mission Completed

I finished the manuscript of this book on August 26, 2024 after Ron and Lib had reviewed a preliminary draft. It was also on the 26th that the manuscript was emailed to the publisher. Later that evening, around 10:00 PM, I received a phone call from Rev. Robert James Jr., our pastor. For him to call that late, I sensed that the reason for his call was not positive. He was calling to tell me that Ron Loftis Sr. had died earlier that day.

The next day, I drove to Hope Mills to visit with Lib. When Stephen, their son, met me at the door, he shared the sequence of Ron's death. Earlier in the day, I had sent Lisa, Ron and Lib's daughter a text saying that the manuscript had been submitted to the publisher and asked that she tell her parents. As I entered the home, Stephen explained that he told Ron that the manuscript had been submitted to the publisher. About 30 minutes after being told about the book, Ron went into the bathroom, but while in there, collapsed to the floor and was lifeless.

Ron had been hospitalized shortly before his death, but when I visited him at their home a few days prior to his death, he was comfortable and alert. Early on, across the months of meeting with Ron and Lib as we discussed their marriage journey, neither of them could understand why I wanted to tell their story. However, I believe that as they had an opportunity to hear and appreciate the course of my marriages and the tremendous help that their story was to me, they came to understand why the book and that it could help others.

Given that Ron came to the point of understanding why I wanted to tell his and Lib's story, I believe that among his reasons for holding on to life was that he wanted this book finished.

Thank you, Ronald Loftis Sr., my genuine friend and exemplary role model.

Karl W. Merritt

ENDNOTES

Chapter One...Why This Book?

[1] "How do individuals generally define a successful marriage?," Scispace, https://typeset.io/questions/how-do-individuals-generally-define-a-successful-marriage-32ldpqnc3c

Chapter Two............................Beginning the Journey to True Love

No References

Chapter Three..Together with God

[1] "Benefits of Believing," Cfaith, (https://www.cfaith.com/index.php/blog/19-articles/faith/21712-benefits-of-believing)

[2] Ronald W. Loftis, Sr., An Unfinished Story: *A Family History from October 7, 1939 through June 30, 2007* (Self-published) 53

[3] Loftis, Sr., An Unfinished Story, 53-54

[4] Loftis, Sr., An Unfinished Story, 46-47

[5] Loftis, Sr., An Unfinished Story, 63-64

[6] Loftis, Sr., An Unfinished Story, 64

[7] Loftis, Sr., An Unfinished Story, 118

[8] Loftis, Sr., An Unfinished Story, 120

Chapter Four...Coming to Grips

[1] "Definitions of 'a grip on reality,'" a grip on reality, Collins, https://collinsdictionary.com/us/dictionary/english/a-grip-on-reality

[2] Peter Scazzero. Emotionally Healthy Spirituality(Grand Rapids: Zondervan, 2017), 9

Chapter Five..........The Bigger Picture of Building a "Strong Family"

1 "Definitions of 'a grip on reality,'" a grip on reality, Collins, https://collinsdictionary.com/us/dictionary/english/a-grip-on-reality

Chapter Six..........................Rearing and Being Blessed by Children

1 Peter Scazzero, *Emotionally Healthy Spirituality* (Zondervan: Grand Rapids, 2017), 91

2 NikkyaHargrove, (2022, March 31). It's Time to Finally Ditch the Stigma Against Stay-at-Home Moms. Healthline. https://www.healthline.com/health/parenting/stigma-stay-at-home-moms#Being-OK- with-not-being-a-stay-at-home-mom

Chapter Seven.......................................Education as a High Priority

1 "Why Education Matters to Health, Exploring the Causes," Center for Society and Health, February 13, 2015. https://www.google.com/search?q=the+importance+of+education+in+our+lives&oq=The+importance+of+education&gs_lcrp=EgZjaHJvbWUqBwgEEAAYgAQyDAgAEAAYQxiABBiKBTIMCAEQABhDGIAEGIoFMgwIAhAAGEMYgAQYigUyBwgDEAAYgAQyBwgEEAAYgAQyBwgFEAAYgAQyBwgGEAAYgAQyBwgHEAAYgAQyBwgIEAAYgAQyBwgJEAAYgATSAQkyODM3OGowajeoAgCwAgA&sourceid=chrome&ie=UTF-8

2 Elizabeth Scott, PhD, "Coping with the Stress Children Add to a Marriage," *verywell mind, January 3, 2023* https://www.verywellmind.com/coping-with-stress-that-children-add-to-marriage-4121318#:~:text=Children%20Reduce%20the%20Likelihood%20of,the%20sake%20of%20their%20children

Chapter Eight..Navigating Conflict

1 "6 Steps for Resolving Conflict in Marriage," Family Life, https://www.familylife.com/articles/topics/marriage/staying-married/resolving-conflict/6-steps-for-resolving-conflict-in-marriage/

2 Ibid

Chapter Nine.............................Core Values Over Shared Interests

1 https://www.google.com/search?q=separate+endeavors+among+married+couples&oq=separate+endeavors+among+married+couples&gs_lcrp=

EgZjaHJvbWUyBggAEEUYOTIHCAEQIRigATIHCAIQIRigATIHCAMQIRigATIHCAQQIRigATIHCAUQIRigATIHCAYQIRirAtIBCTM5Mzk1ajBqN6gCALACAA&sourceid=chrome&ie=UTF-8

2 https://www.google.com/search?q=values+in+a+relationship&oq=Values+in+a+relationship&gs_lcrp=EgZjaHJvbWUqCQgAEEUYOxiABDIJCAAQRRg7GIAEMgcIARAAGIAEMgcIAhAAGIAEMgcIAxAAGIAEMgcIBBAAGIAEMgcIBRAAGIAEMgcIBhAAGIAEMggIBxAAGBYYHjIICAgQABgWGB4yCAgJEAAYFhgeqAIAsAIA&sourceid=chrome&ie=UTF-8

3 https://www.google.com/search?q=description+of+the+laubach+reading+program&oq=Description+of+the+Lauback+&gs_lcrp=EgZjaHJvbWUqCQgBECEYChigATIGCAAQRRg5MgkIARAhGAoYoAEyCQgCECEYChigATIHCAMQIRirAtIBCTE3MDczajBqN6gCALACAA&sourceid=chrome&ie=UTF-8

4 "Mission Statement," Woman's Missionary Union of North Carolina, https://www.wmunc.org/

5 Zeta Norwood, "Is Marital Stress Impacting Your Ability to Focus at Work? Then Read This." Linked in, August 30, 2016. https://www.linkedin.com/pulse/how-improve-your-marriage-save-career-zeta-yarwood-

Chapter Ten........................Positively Touching the Lives of Others

1 Ashlynn Larsen, "The Importance of Love on Well Being," My Best Self 101, February 20,2024, https://www.mybestself101.org/blog/the-importance-of-love-onwellbeing#:~:text=The%20benefits%20of%20love%20extend,associated%20with%20resilience%20and%20longevity.

2 Ibid

3 Ibid.

Chapter Eleven..................Vivian...The Ultimate in Shared Ministry

1 Susan Mathis, "Serving Together as a Couple," Focus on the Family, January 1, 2011, https://www.focusonthefamily.com/marriage/serving-together-as-a-couple/

Chapter Twelve...Growing Old Together

1 "Conscious aging: How to accept and enjoy life at every stage," Piedmont, https://www.piedmont.org/living-real-change/conscious-aging-how-to-accept-and-enjoy-life-at-every-stage

www.ingramcontent.com/pod-product-compliance
Lightning Source LLC
LaVergne TN
LVHW041712060526
838201LV00043B/689